DEAD FAMOUS

Joan of Arc

AND HER MARCHING ORDERS

by **Phil Robins**

Illustrated by Philip Reeve

Hippo

Scholastic Children's Books,
Commonwealth House, 1–19 New Oxford Street,
London WC1A 1NU, UK

A division of Scholastic Ltd
London ~ New York ~ Toronto ~ Sydney ~ Auckland
Mexico City ~ New Delhi ~ Hong Kong

Published in the UK by Scholastic Ltd, 2002

Text copyright © Phil Robins, 2002
Illustrations copyright © Philip Reeve, 2002

ISBN 0 439 98110 7

Typeset by M Rules
Printed and bound in Great Britain by Cox & Wyman Ltd,
Reading, Berkshire

2 4 6 8 10 9 7 5 3 1

CONTENTS

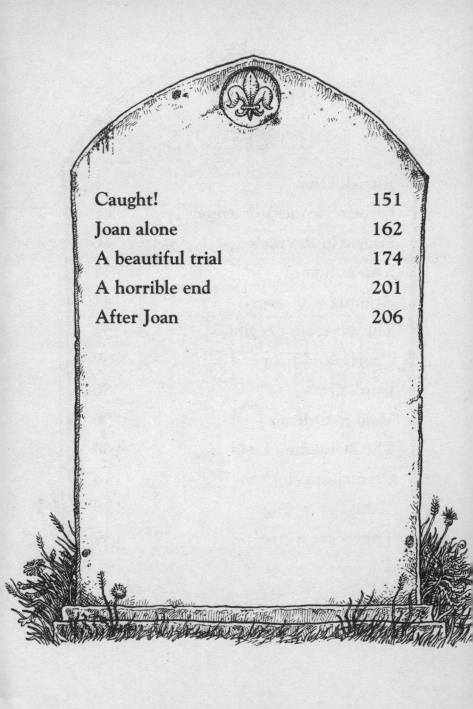

INTRODUCTION

Most people have heard of Joan of Arc, but why exactly is she dead famous?

SHE'S A SAINT!

SHE LED AN ARMY!

SHE WAS BURNT AT THE STAKE!

SHE HEARD VOICES!

In fact, Joan started out as a very ordinary peasant girl. She grew up working on her dad's farm and at first she didn't seem anything special at all. To get *anywhere* in her day, you really needed to be a man, and also rich – but Joan wasn't either of those things. And yet she ended up changing the course of her country's history and becoming the most famous and successful military leader of her day – and all this when she was only *seventeen years old*. So how did she manage to have such a big impact?

Well, for one thing, Joan knew how to speak her mind. She was always getting cross about what was going on in the world around her; and she often wrote to kings and dukes and other important types, telling them how to put things right and giving them their marching orders.

ANOTHER LETTER FROM JOAN, SIRE...

But she didn't just send her letters and leave it at that: thanks to a king-sized temper, a taste for action-packed adventure and a never-say-die attitude, more often than not she got her way.

Incredibly, Joan went from minding sheep and cattle to supping with kings and leading armies into battle, and this book tells you how she did it. You'll read all about the strange angelic voices she heard and the extraordinary things they told her. You'll have the chance to make up your own mind about some of the miraculous things she's supposed to have done. You'll find out how she coped under the spotlight in one of the most sensational trials of all time. And you'll hear more about Joan's sad and smoky end.

There are some surprises, too. For instance, did you know. . .

- she had to run away from home to go and meet the King of France?
- she tried to stop a whole army from swearing?

- she survived a crossbow bolt through her chest?
- she stole a bishop's horse?

Joan's story is often told as though it were a fairy tale: something that happened once upon a time in a land far, far away. . . But, as you'll see, Joan was a very down-to-earth girl – if a bit unusual. (OK, sometimes she was downright strange.) Anyway, what happened to her was very real, and her story certainly had no fairy-tale ending.

Over the centuries, people have told Joan's story hundreds of times. She's starred in more books and films than almost anyone else in history. And she's *never* failed to impress. Read on and find out why. . .

FARMER JACQUES'S DAUGHTER

In 1431 the 19-year-old Joan of Arc was all alone as she faced those who accused her across the courtroom. In the last couple of years she'd achieved many unlikely things – almost impossible things. She'd won battles, crowned a king and saved her country. But now her luck had run out, her extraordinary adventures were over, and she was in the hands of her enemies.

During the trial, Joan faced a barrage of questions about her past. Where had she been born? Who were her parents? What had she been like as a child? Above all else, her enemies wanted to know this: *Who was this girl who'd caused them so much trouble?*

Joan answered these questions honestly: she had nothing to hide. And other witnesses later backed up what Joan said. It's mainly because of these answers, which were carefully written down at the time, that we know how Joan's story began. . .

Baby Joan

No one's *exactly* sure of the date but baby Joan was probably born on a cold January night in 1412, in a tiny little village called Domrémy, in eastern France. Domrémy is in the middle of the beautiful region known as Lorraine (where the quiche comes from).

Joan's proud mum and dad were a hard-working couple called Jacques and Isabelle Darc.

Armed with the facts

Joan's name

Joan (or Jeanne in French) became known as Joan 'of Arc' by mistake. Her family name was Darc, but some people wrongly thought this was 'd'Arc' short for 'de Arc' which means 'of (or from) Arc'. So the person we know as 'Joan of Arc' was really Jeanne Darc of Domrémy!

Jacques Darc owned a medium-sized farm in Domrémy, and Isabelle helped him by looking after the house and the children, as well as by spinning and sewing to make a little extra money. Jacques Darc was quite an important man in Domrémy and was next in charge after the mayor and the sheriff. (Mind you, it was only a very small village.)

Because of her dad's important position, Joan grew up in one of Domrémy's slightly cosier cottages whose walls were made of bricks (and not mud like many of the others). Joan even had her own tiny bedroom. Still, the cottage was fairly basic by today's standards.[1]

Life in the Darc household must have been quite lively. Joan also had three brothers and a sister, and of course there were loads of animals to look after too.

1. Joan's cottage is still standing today, and is part of a big museum devoted to Joan that's visited by people from all over the world.

Troubled times

Domrémy was a beautiful little village, and might have been a nice place to grow up if times had been better. But for families like the Darcs, there was a big black cloud constantly on the horizon. For many years, France had been involved in a terrible war, and large parts of the country, including Lorraine, were occupied by enemy soldiers.

Fortunately, Lorraine wasn't an especially important region, and there wasn't all that much fighting there compared with some other areas. On the whole, villagers in places like Domrémy were left in peace.

Even so, soldiers frequently passed through on their way to fight battles elsewhere and although they usually did so without causing trouble, they weren't always well-behaved – sometimes far from it. Now and then villages like Domrémy would be attacked by passing soldiers. Sometimes they'd even be burnt to the ground.

Down on the farm

As well as having to worry about the war, just making a living on the land meant a lot of hard work for the villagers of Domrémy. Life wasn't easy in those days, and like the rest of her family, little Joan had to pull her weight on the farm.

Being a girl, Joan also had to help her mum with the spinning and sewing, and during her later adventures she would fondly remember the many hours they'd spent sitting and chatting while they worked. (Even after she became famous and was mixing with royalty, Joan often liked to tell people what a dab hand she was with a needle and thread.) It was during this time that her mum taught Joan how to say her prayers and warned her over and over again to keep away from soldiers.

School's out

What with one thing and another, Joan wouldn't have had time for school, even if there'd been one in Domrémy. But in those days it was only rich nobles who had the chance to become educated. Poor villagers had to make do without. That's why Joan never even learnt to read or write.

With no school to go to, Joan would have learnt everything she needed to know from her family and friends in the village. So what sort of report might they have given her?

Progress report: Joan Darc, aged 8	
French:	Excellent. Joan already speaks French like a native. (Of course the fact that she is French helps a lot.).
Maths:	Good. Joan can do sums as long as they're just adding up ones (i.e. she can count her father's sheep).

Geography:	Very good. Joan is capable of finding her way round the village all by herself, and knows quite a lot about farming ...
Sewing:	Excellent. Joan can mend socks till the cows come home (when she has to milk them).
Games:	Good. When playing in the fields with the other village children Joan is a fierce competitor and doesn't like to admit defeat (especially when the game is fighting).
Religious Education:	Very good. Joan knows a lot of prayers by heart and likes going to church.

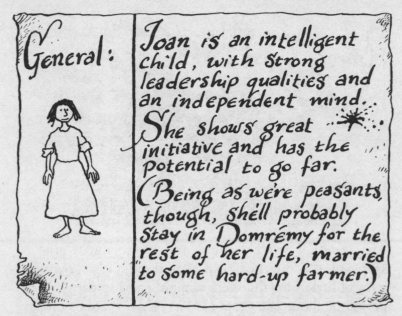

General: Joan is an intelligent child, with strong leadership qualities and an independent mind... She shows great initiative and has the potential to go far. (Being as we're peasants, though, she'll probably stay in Domrémy for the rest of her life, married to some hard-up farmer.)

As we know though, Joan *didn't* just do what was expected of her and settle down to a quiet life. Instead, she made her mark on history. This was all because of the war, which is what Joan got cross about more than anything else. So before we go on with Joan's story, let's find out a bit more about it...

15

SQUATCH!

DOINK!

FRANCE IN THE WARS

The war that was causing everybody so much grief is known as the Hundred Years War, though it was actually a lot of little wars that kept stopping and starting over a period of about 116 years (1337–1453). France's enemy was England, but all the fighting took place in France itself, so French people suffered a lot more.

Basically, the English went over to France, smashed the place up, killed people left, right and centre and stole all their money. And they didn't just do it once, they did it over and over again. Here's how one French writer, who lived at the time, described them:

> *They are an accursed race, opposed to all good and all reason, ravening wolves, proud, arrogant hypocrites, tricksters without any conscience . . . men who drink and gorge on human blood, with natures like birds of prey, people who live only by plunder.*

AND THAT'S PUTTING IT MILDLY!

How it all started

In 1328 the King of France died without any sons, so his crown passed to his French cousin instead, which was fair enough, most people thought. . . But Edward III of England was also a relation – his mum was the dead King's sister – so he decided *he* ought to be King of France (as well as England).

PAH! BEING KING OF ONLY ONE COUNTRY IS FOR LOSERS!

Armed with the facts

France and England

The French and the English had been bickering over territory for years. In 1066 the Normans had come from France and invaded the Saxons in England. They'd stayed there for centuries and come to think of themselves as English (though the posh ones still spoke some French). It's partly why the English descendants of the Norman invaders, including Edward III, thought they had a right to rule in France, since that's where they were from originally. Even before the Hundred Years War, the English owned bits of land in the area we now think of as 'France' and naturally this led to arguments.

Edward soon got an army together and crossed the Channel in 1337 to wreak havoc in France. Later English kings followed in Edward's footsteps and over the next hundred years or so going to France and acting like a complete hooligan was very much the done thing among the English upper classes. English kings rewarded posh English lords who fought for them with land in France, and before long anybody who was anybody in England owned a bit of France as well.

Cut down to size

By the time Joan was born in 1412, the English were in control of a large chunk of northern France (Normandy). The French, it turned out, weren't especially good at fighting off the English bullies and they kept getting beaten in important battles. . .

THE GALLIC GLOBE

August 1346

CRUSHED AT CRÉCY

Reports are coming in that our entire army has been virtually wiped out by the evil English. Crécy will be remembered as a complete disaster for France.

THE GALLIC GLOBE

September 1356

POUNDED AT POITIERS

give him back in exchange for about a third of his territory.

After giving us another complete thrashing, this time at the Battle of Poitiers, the English have actually captured our king! Sacré bleu! And the cheeky blighters are holding him to ransom! They will only give him back in exchange for about a third of his territory.

We French have decided to cough up (well, we can't really do without him, can we?), so he'll soon be ruling a much smaller kingdom than he does today.

There was a brief lull for a few years while everyone caught their breath. (The new English king, Richard II, preferred reading poetry and painting watercolours to making war.) But eventually Henry V became King of England, and things got even worse. He liked nothing better than organizing jolly sprees of murder and mayhem overseas and he made it his life's work to take over France once and for all.

THE GALLIC GLOBE

October 1415

ANNIHILATED AT AGINCOURT

Zut alors! Guess what? We've been stuffed again, this time at the Battle of Agincourt – a complete bloodbath in which 10,000 Frenchmen were killed, but only 300 English. Now the kingdom of France is titchier than ever.

Plots, schemes and power games

In such difficult times, the French really needed a strong king to guide them. But for some years they'd been out of luck. . .

THE GALLIC GLOBE

August 1392

KING IS BARMY!

King Charles VI, who has suffered under the strain of recent events, is now thought to be absolutely stark staring mad.

Doubts about the king's mental health were first aroused earlier this year when he shot a number of his own men while out riding.

They were confirmed more recently when he was spotted running around his castle smashing plates, breaking furniture and howling like a wolf.

Yesterday he forbade doctors to come anywhere near him, claiming to be made of glass which would break if anyone touched him.

His condition is said to be extremely fragile.

With poor old Charles the Mad (as he later became known) too potty to rule France properly, other people tried to do it for him. (You couldn't just get rid of a mad king in those days, but you could try to keep him on the sidelines.) The main players in this power game were. . .

**Queen Isabella,
Charles's wife**
At first she was upset about her husband's illness, but soon turned to others to help her rule.

**Louis, Duke of Orléans,
Charles's brother**
Wanted to carry on fighting the English, hoping one of Charles VI and Isabella's sons would one day rule France.

**John the Fearless,
Duke of Burgundy**
Preferred to make peace with England, secretly hoping that he and they might one day divide up France between them.

Armed with the facts
Burgundy
Burgundy was really just a region of France, and in the past, the Dukes of Burgundy had been loyal to their ruler, the King of France. But over the years the French king had rewarded them with more and more land. They'd got more and more powerful, and now even owned land *outside* France.

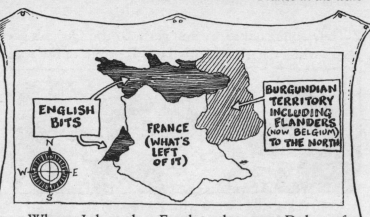

When John the Fearless became Duke of Burgundy he soon began to act like he was ruler of a separate country, and didn't always side with France at all. (He was friendly with the English partly because Flanders did lots of trade with them.)

Anyway, here's what happened:

1 John and Louis hated each other's guts, and were always squabbling.

2 They competed to try and get into the Queen's good books while Charles the Mad was kept out of the way.

3 At first Isabella flirted with Louis.

4 Until he was brutally murdered in 1407.

5 Eventually, Isabella decided that John was better placed to help her rule (what with him being still alive, and everything).

Isabella didn't want to be on the losing side, whatever happened. And in the end it seemed safest to be extra-friendly with John the Fearless and get her dotty old hubby to try and make peace with the English rather than try to fight them any more.

France divided

As a result of the rivalry between John and Louis, the people of France had split into two warring factions. Those who'd been fans of Louis took the name 'Armagnacs' (after the Duke of Armagnac, their new leader). Those who rooted for the Duke of Burgundy became known as 'Burgundians' (even though they were from France not Burgundy).

ᴀRMAGNACS	BURGUNDIANS
◉ WANT ONE OF CHARLES THE MAD'S SONS TO RULE FRANCE.	◈ WANT DUKE OF BURGUNDY TO RULE BITS OF FRANCE LEFT OVER BY ENGLISH.
◉ WANT TO FIGHT THE ENGLISH AND THE BURGUNDIANS.	◈ WANT TO MAKE PEACE WITH THE ENGLISH AND CRUSH THE ARMAGNACS.
◉ MOSTLY IN SOUTH-WEST OF FRANCE.	◈ MOSTLY IN NORTH-EAST OF FRANCE.

The two sides fought fiercely for years, but in the end peace talks seemed like a good idea – otherwise the English might take advantage of the feuding and overrun France completely. (Not even the Burgundians wanted *that*.) So, one day, John the Fearless received an invitation from some of the top Armagnac leaders. . .

Dear Mr Fearless (our hated enemy),

We know you killed Louis a few years ago and are very friendly with our arch-enemies, the English. Still, for the sake of our country, we are willing to forgive and forget. Why not come and meet us on the bridge at Montéreau (on 10th September 1419) so we can ~~kill you~~. KISS AND MAKE UP.

Your trustworthy friends,
The Armagnac Leaders.

Please Bring A ~~Coffin~~ BOTTLE.

Instead of RSVPing that he was washing his hair that night, John lived up to his name and went. He thought the Armagnacs would try and tempt him to swap sides and join them against the English by promising him lots of money and power. But, instead, an argument developed . . . which turned into a scuffle . . . and a few moments later. . .

The Armagnacs had finally got their revenge for the murder of Louis. But it didn't look good sending John home from the peace talks with a pickaxe through his skull – and the results were disastrous.

Armed with the facts

Whodunnit?

The main person John had gone to talk to on the bridge was a sixteen-year-old boy named Charles, who was one of Charles VI's and Isabella's sons and who hoped to be King of France one day. He wasn't a very strong or decisive person, as we'll see, and it probably wasn't his idea to kill John. (It almost certainly wasn't him who did it.) Still, Charles got the blame so he ran away and hid.

Later, his mother Isabella disowned Charles completely, and she and her Burgundian friends tried to convince people he was a murderer who didn't deserve to be king. (Some people even said his dad wasn't Charles VI at all, but one of Isabella's boyfriends, which would mean the young Charles didn't have royal blood.)

Horrified by the Armagnacs' treachery, the Burgundians now made a much firmer alliance with the English against them. And Isabella now teamed up with the new Duke of Burgundy, a chap by the name of Philip the Good.

WELL, GOOD-ISH...

The two of them were determined that the Armagnacs should be defeated once and for all, even if it meant doing a deal which handed the French crown to the English.

The treacherous Treaty of Troyes

When it became obvious Charles the Mad was about to pop his clogs, Isabella and her new friend Philip the Good forced him to sign a treaty with Henry V of England:

TREATY OF TROYES 1420

~~My wife says~~ I mean I hereby declare that my daughter will marry my worst enemy, King Henry of England, who will also look after my country for me from now on. When I die, their son (who isn't even born yet) will be King of France and not my grown-up son, Charles (even though he is the rightful heir as well as being French into the bargain). Seems fair enough to me.

~~The Tooth Fairy~~
King Charles VI

English kings had claimed a right to the French crown for years, but so far French kings had always told them to get stuffed. (Even though they'd lost a lot of battles, they'd never admitted complete defeat.) But now a barmy French king had actually signed away his kingdom!

The Armagnacs were furious about the Treaty of Troyes, and thought it was nonsense. And all over France – including the village of Domrémy – many people agreed.

JOAN AT HOME

To Joan and her family, the political drama must have seemed fairly remote. News travelled slowly in those days – it wasn't beamed into people's living rooms as it happened – and people in villages like Domrémy would have had only a rough idea of what was going on.

Still, as we've seen, the soldiers who passed by and threatened to attack Lorraine villages were real enough. These soldiers were mostly Burgundian, because Lorraine was right in the middle of Burgundian-held territory.

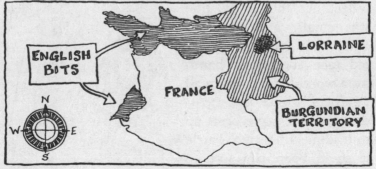

Although most of the villages in Lorraine supported the Burgundians, there were pockets of Armagnac support too, and Domrémy was one of these. Like France as a whole, the area was deeply divided by the war, so neighbouring villages could find themselves on opposite sides.

On the whole, villagers in Lorraine were too busy trying to make a living on the land to mess about fighting with their neighbours. Mostly they just put up with each other and left the murder and mayhem to the soldiers. Mind you, they couldn't always stop the children from picking fights. . .

A down-to-earth girl

Joan of Arc is often pictured as a pale, elegant beauty – a bit like a fairy-tale princess – but she almost certainly wasn't like that at all. She was small, and probably quite plain-looking, with a red face and rough hands from working outdoors in all weathers. Good job too – she wouldn't have been up to leading armies into battle if she'd been the sort to worry about broken nails and split ends.

And she certainly didn't act like a fairy-tale princess. She could be a bit of a loudmouth, for a start, and was always a very straight talker. For example, when she got cross with someone – like the one troublemaker in Domrémy who said he supported the Burgundians not the Armagnacs – she often told them she'd like to see their head chopped off! But Joan wasn't really a bloodthirsty girl, it was just her blunt way of talking.

Away with the fairies
Frightening the living daylights out of people wasn't the only way to have fun, though, and when she had time off from her chores, Joan sometimes went off with her best friends – two girls called Hauviette and Mengette – to explore the oldest part of the forest, the ancient oakwood. According to a local superstition, fairies lived here, and next to a spring that was meant to have magical healing powers was an old tree known as the Fairies' Tree. (Legend had it that a knight used to come here to chat up one of the lady fairies.)

Children from Domrémy often brought a picnic and danced round the tree, singing songs and hanging flowers on its branches as a present to the fairies. The villagers knew these old superstitions were nonsense, but they didn't want to stop the children enjoying themselves, and everyone agreed it was all just a bit of harmless fun. (Little did anyone know that one day it would cause trouble for Joan.)

Holy Joan

On Sundays, Joan and her family always put on their best smocks and went to church with all the other villagers.

𝕸𝖊𝖉𝖎𝖊𝖛𝖆𝖑 𝕸𝖆𝖙𝖙𝖊𝖗𝖘

Going to church

Nowadays most people prefer to spend their Sundays washing the car, cutting the grass or hanging about in DIY superstores on the outskirts of town. In the Middle Ages, though, going to church was a must. In fact, *not* going to church was more or less unthinkable. The Christian religion was an important part of life for everyone in medieval France. Times were hard and people could expect to die fairly young. The Church offered them comfort and support in the face of death and disaster.

Even in those days, though, some people were more keen on going to church than others. Joan was absolutely mad about it and sometimes got in trouble for going too often!

The church in Domrémy was right next door to Joan's dad's house, and Joan loved the musical sound of its bells, announcing the Hours of Prayer. She always made a point of listening out for them wherever she was in the village and once, when the church warden dozed off and didn't ring them, Joan gave him a sharp ticking off for not doing his duty. She even tried to bribe him with little presents if he promised to do better in future!

Another reason Joan liked church was because it kept her in touch with what was going on. In those days, it was probably at church where everyone was gathered together that villagers heard the latest rumours about the war. . .

And then, of course, there was the church service itself. In those days services were mostly in Latin and even though she didn't always understand exactly what was being said, Joan liked to hear the priest murmuring the mysterious-sounding words. Above all, Joan enjoyed taking communion and confessing her sins. . .

𝔐𝔢𝔡𝔦𝔢𝔳𝔞𝔩 𝔐𝔞𝔱𝔱𝔢𝔯𝔰

Communion
Communion was the really important bit of the church service when you ate a bit of bread and sip some wine. These had been specially blessed by the priest so that they became the body and blood of Christ, given for the forgiveness of sins.

Confession
Confession means going to a priest and telling him all the bad things you've been up to so God can forgive you.

Another thing about church was that it fired Joan's imagination. Because she didn't go to school, and never learnt to read or write, the pictures and stories she saw and heard in the church at Domrémy were really important to her. These were about saints and angels and battles between Good and Evil and Joan quickly came to see the war in France in these terms. She felt sure that God must be appalled by the injustice of the war and must soon help France to conquer her enemies.

36

New developments

God didn't seem to be listening to Joan's prayers, though, because when she was about ten years old, the English stranglehold on France became stronger than ever...

THE BURGUNDIAN BUGLE

22nd October 1422

BONKERS KING KICKS THE BUCKET

OUR ENGLISH FRIENDS
NOW IN CHARGE

Charles the Mad is dead at last. And, as everyone knows, King Henry V of England pegged out earlier this year too (God rest his soul). So, according to the marvellous Treaty of Troyes, Henry's son (Henry VI) is now king of England *and* France.

He's a tiny bit short of experience, it must be said, since he isn't yet two years old!

So, until he's grown up a bit, a top English noble, the Duke of Bedford, will look after France for him, helped by his ally the Duke of Burgundy (our wonderful leader).

This paper says: Hurray. The country is in safe hands at last.

INSIDE: LEARN TO SPEAK ENGLISH! *FREE!*
Includes: "Hello", "Goodbye", "I surrender", "Please stop hitting me" and many other handy phrases.

For the Armagnacs, things looked pretty bleak. But hold on a minute. Surely this wasn't *all* bad news?

THE ARMAGNAC NEWS

October 1422

OUR CHANCE AT LAST?

Everyone knows the Treaty of Troyes is poppycock. Now the mad King who signed it is dead and gone (God bless him), the way is surely clear for his son to take over as the new French king. And with the new English King still in his nappies (even if he does have grown-up nobles to help him), it won't be hard for our man to get the upper hand.

It just remains to be seen how our gallant new King will rise to the challenge.

So who was the new French hope? Well, Charles the Mad had had several sons, and the Armagnacs had expected one of them to make a good strong king. But by 1422 all of them had died except the youngest, who was called Charles after his dad. (He was the chap who'd gone to meet John the Fearless on the bridge at Montereau, and who'd run away after some people had blamed him for John's murder.)

As we've seen, many Armagnac people in France expected much from their 20-year-old Dauphin Charles. (Dauphin is pronounced "dough-fan" and was what the French called a prince who was due to inherit the crown.) Few had seen him, of course, and most people had no idea what he was like. (No photos or TV pics in those days!) But if they imagined some handsome hero who would lead them to victory they couldn't have been more wrong!

In fact, Charles was a nervous wreck and was afraid to do *anything* by himself. So although the Armagnacs thought he was now their king, and not just Dauphin, he didn't even have the courage to go and get himself crowned properly, which would have shown everyone that he really *believed* he was king. Instead, he just tried to lie low and avoid too much attention! (We'll find out more about him later.)

Meanwhile. . .

Since Joan never learned to read or write, she couldn't have written a diary. But if she'd dictated one, like she later did with her letters, maybe it would have looked like this. . .

JOAN'S SECRET DIARY

Summer 1423

There are rumours that Domrémy could be raided any day. Dad says we might have to run away to another village.

Personally, I'd like to stay and give those soldiers a piece of my mind! But no one takes any notice of me; I'm only eleven.

—AND ANOTHER THING...

When <u>is</u> our Dauphin Charles going to do something to save us? And when's he going to get crowned as king and fight the English properly? Oh well, I suppose he knows what he's doing — he is the Dauphin, after all.

Well, I should really be getting on with my work now, though it's a bit dull. Cows are all right, but they don't say a lot. There's always God to talk to, I suppose. But, to be honest, He doesn't say much either. _I wish He would talk to me._

ARGUING WITH ANGELS

By the time Joan was about 13 she'd become a bit of a loner. She often went wandering off into the woods on her own to think and pray, sometimes forgetting all about the animals she was supposed to be minding.

OH YES, THAT'S RIGHT. OFF YOU GO. DON'T MIND US.

YEAH, HAVE A NICE PRAY.

One of her favourite walks was a long uphill climb through the forest to a little deserted chapel that she knew about. There she'd kneel in front of the statue of the Virgin Mary and pray for hours at a time in the silence. She'd come home late and wouldn't tell her parents where she'd been.

Her friends noticed that Joan wasn't always joining in with their games like she used to, and they would often see her walking around with a strange far-away look on her face.

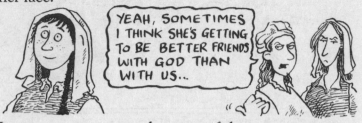

YEAH, SOMETIMES I THINK SHE'S GETTING TO BE BETTER FRIENDS WITH GOD THAN WITH US...

Joan spent more and more of her time going to confession, too, which wasn't a top priority for most 13-year-olds, even in those days.

Then, one day, something happened that was to change Joan's life for ever.

JOAN'S SECRET DIARY (aged 13½)
Domrémy, August 1425

Today something incredible has happened. I think God has actually spoken to me.

I was racing in the field with the other kids. I hadn't eaten all day, and it was boiling hot, and after the race I thought I was going to faint so I lay down on the grass for a breather and shut my eyes.

Then I heard a voice — I thought it must have been one of the boys — saying my mum needed me. So I rushed home. But when I got there Mum

said she hadn't asked for me at all.
So I ran off through Dad's garden towards the pastures. It was about midday and on my right towards the church there was a patch of bright light. I stopped and rubbed my eyes, and I started to get really scared. And then I heard a voice, a man's voice, coming from the patch of light.

It was the most beautiful voice I've ever heard, and I'll never forget it for as long as I live. It said, 'Joan, be a good girl: go often to church.'
I was too surprised to say anything, and before long the light had gone and I was all alone again. Later I thought about the whole thing and decided it must have been the voice of God.

Did Joan really hear God speaking to her through an angel? Or was she just imagining it? Did it happen because she hadn't eaten all day and it was very hot and she felt faint after running? Was it what today we might call a hallucination, something that she thought she saw and heard but which didn't really exist except in her own head?

It's often said that people who spend too much time on their own are more likely to start seeing things (and hearing them). Joan was often alone, and she was also an imaginative child, who desperately wanted God to speak to her. Did she want it so badly that her own mind made it happen?

Joan didn't think so. As far as she was concerned her prayers to God had quite literally been answered. And her conversation with God had only just begun.

Joan's big secret

It wasn't long before Joan heard the voice again. And what the voice said to her this time was really incredible. He told her to go and help the King of France fight his enemies!

Joan was to have many, many more days like this. The voice kept coming back to her and telling her the same thing. And every time, Joan pointed out that this was an impossible task for a 13-year-old girl to perform. But she would hear the voice more and more often, at least three times a week and sometimes even several times a day. She'd hear it in her father's garden at noon, in the woods in the afternoon, and most often in the fields in the evening when the church bells were ringing in the distance.

Gradually, as the months passed, the voice seemed to Joan to take on a more definite personality, and in the end she would recognize it as the Archangel Saint Michael. Before long he was joined by two other voices, telling her the same thing, and these she would eventually recognized as Saint Catherine and Saint Margaret.

These three legendary characters were like celebrities in the Middle Ages, as well known as some pop stars are today. And as you can see from these profiles, they also had a lot of connections with Lorraine, so Joan would have known plenty about them. . .

ARCHANGEL SAINT MICHAEL

Mike's career began spectacularly well when, back in the early days of creation, he led God's army of angels against bad-apple Archangel Lucifer and successfully kicked him and his followers out of heaven into hell (where Lucifer now rules as the Devil). Since then Mike has been one of God's most trusted and respected angels all over the world.

Favourite clothes:
Shiny suit of golden armour and long sword.

Favourite music:
Military marches and heavenly tunes.

Favourite country:
France, where the Armagnacs have adopted him as an emblem of resistance.

Do say:
'I really love your early work.'

Don't say:
'Be an angel and fetch my slippers.'

SAINT CATHERINE

In the third century AD Catherine was a king's daughter who had the bottle to argue with an evil emperor. Things spiralled out of control, however, when he punished her by tying her to a wheel and spinning it round really fast. Once she was beheaded, however, she never looked back. Now a fully-fledged saint, she went on to become very big in Europe as heavenly protector of young girls. More recently she made an explosive comeback when she launched her new career as a firework, the much-loved Catherine Wheel.

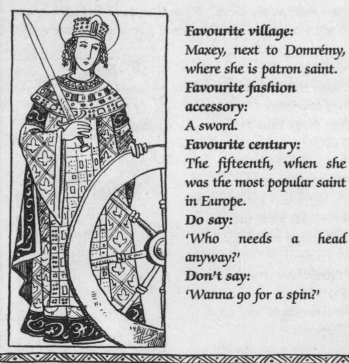

Favourite village:
Maxey, next to Domrémy, where she is patron saint.
Favourite fashion accessory:
A sword.
Favourite century:
The fifteenth, when she was the most popular saint in Europe.
Do say:
'Who needs a head anyway?'
Don't say:
'Wanna go for a spin?'

SAINT MARGARET

Legend has it that Margaret was a shepherdess who fell on hard times after throwing herself from a high tower rather than be forced to take a husband. She survived, and proved her staying-power when she was swallowed whole

by a dragon and then sicked up again alive and well. You just can't keep a good woman down! She too was beheaded before establishing a successful career as patron saint of pregnant women and people possessed by demons.

Hobbies:
Wearing men's clothes from time to time. (She thought it put men off wanting to marry her.)
Favourite fashion accessory:
A sword.
Favourite church:
The one at Domrémy where a statue of Margaret, made in the early fifteenth century, still stands today.
Do say:
'So what's it like being swallowed by a dragon, then?'
Don't say:
'Will you marry me?'

Joan's voices spoke to her so often that eventually she got to know them better than her friends and family. Later, Joan said she could hear them, see them, and even smell them! (At her trial Joan said Catherine and Margaret had such a lovely perfumy fragrance that she couldn't bear it when they vanished without taking her with them.) Much as she loved them, though, she still thought what they were saying was ridiculous, and trying to talk sense into her voices was soon a regular part of Joan's day.

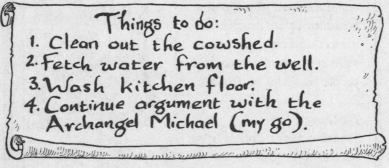

There must have been times when she didn't know whether she was coming or going, what with all the different voices telling her what to do.

𝕸𝖊𝖉𝖎𝖊𝖛𝖆𝖑 𝕸𝖆𝖙𝖙𝖊𝖗𝖘

Hearing voices

Nowadays we tend to think somebody is crackers if they claim to hear voices no one else can. In the Middle Ages, though, such claims were taken more seriously. Every now and then a mystic or saint would turn up saying that they'd heard the voice of God, and people often believed them. But people thought the Devil could speak too, and they were terrified that if someone heard a voice it might be the Devil, perhaps tricking them into doing something wicked by pretending to be a voice from God.

Sometimes Joan was scared that she might be wrong about her voices. Perhaps they weren't from God at all, but from the Devil. If she *were* to go and help Charles, for instance, she'd have to desert her poor old mum and dad who needed her help at home. Perhaps the Devil was tempting her to do the wrong thing? With worries like these, it's not surprising Joan spent such a long time arguing with her voices. Joan was a strong-willed girl and she wasn't about to abandon her parents and march off on some reckless adventure just because a voice told her to. She didn't want to disobey God, but she had to make absolutely sure it was God she was dealing with!

In all, Joan spoke to her voices for an incredible *three years* before she acted! No one could say that Joan was a pushover!

To tell or not to tell

Finally when she was 16, Joan gave in. Her voices were now giving her some practical tips, and advised her that she should ask the local Armagnac captain for help. He was called Captain Baudricourt, and was based at a town called Vaucouleurs, about 12 miles away. (Joan may have heard of Captain Baudricourt from her dad, who as deputy-deputy-mayor would probably have met him on official village business.) Baudricourt, the voices said, would take her to the Dauphin, and Joan decided to give it a go.

Should she tell her parents she planned to approach the captain? The trouble was she couldn't imagine them taking her very seriously...

So Joan tried to keep her plans a secret.

It wasn't easy, though, and she must have been busting to tell someone. (Hearing voices could be a very lonely business!) Perhaps she did drop a few hints around the village because one day her dad seems to have got wind something was up. He told her he'd had a dream in which Joan had decided to go off with a lot of soldiers. (He was certainly getting warm, but probably had the wrong end of the stick and thought she was after a snog.) He was furious and told her he'd rather drown her in a pond than let that happen!

Joan realized she'd have to lie to her parents, which must have upset her a lot. Nevertheless she was determined to leave home, and it wasn't long before she got her chance. . .

51

THE ADVENTURE BEGINS
(AFTER A COUPLE OF HICCUPS)

Joan's mum had a cousin, a woman who lived a couple of miles outside Vaucouleurs. Joan got on well with her, and also with her husband, a labourer called Durand Lassois. In the summer of 1428 Joan persuaded her parents to let her go and stay for a week with this couple whom she liked to call 'Aunt' and 'Uncle'.

Uncle Durand thought the world of Joan, and would have done anything for her, so she soon got him to agree to take her to Baudricourt.

Getting an old softie like Uncle Durand to take her a couple of miles was one thing, but Captain Baudricourt was a tough-talking, no-nonsense army captain, and Joan had a much bigger favour to ask him. She must have been incredibly nervous as Uncle Durand introduced her to the captain, but she kept her cool and carefully explained why she was there. . .

And that's exactly what happened.

Back to the drawing board

Mr and Mrs Darc must have been really worried about their daughter's behaviour. No doubt they'd have liked a nice young man from Domrémy to marry her as soon as possible, and with any luck keep her under his thumb. And in fact it was around this time that Joan found herself summoned to a local court, falsely accused of once promising to tie the knot with a young man from a nearby village and then changing her mind. (In those days girls weren't allowed to break engagements, unless the man agreed.) But Joan, who had never promised anything of the sort, went to the court and spoke in her own defence.

No one knows who cooked up this plan to marry Joan off, but we do know that it failed miserably. She spoke out so firmly that the charges were soon dropped. What's more, everybody realized what a tough customer Joan could be.

It was around this time, too, that Joan's family and some of the other villagers had to run away from Domrémy for a few weeks, because it was attacked by soldiers. They stayed in a nearby town called Neufchâteau, where Joan and her friend Hauviette got jobs doing the washing-up in a local inn.

Later that year, as Joan was moping about at Domrémy, wondering how she could get to the Dauphin, news came that the English were now besieging the city of Orléans, the most important Armagnac stronghold of all.

Armed with the Facts

Sieges

A siege is when one army surrounds a town or city belonging to their enemies. (Medieval towns and cities had protective walls round them.) They try to stop food and supplies getting in so that the town or city is forced to surrender.

JOAN'S SECRET DIARY (aged 16)

Domrémy, December 1428

Everyone says that if Orléans falls it will be a complete disaster. And my voices agree, though they seem to think I can prevent it.

Last night they said: 'Go to the Dauphin, <u>save Orléans</u>, and then lead the Dauphin to be crowned.'

Oh dear, the list of things I'm supposed to do just keeps getting longer!

How on earth am I going to save Orléans? Well, I'll just have to cross that bridge when I get to it, I suppose. My voices must know what they're talking about.

First things first, I <u>must</u> get to the Dauphin before it's too late. I can't do <u>anything</u> without him.

Luckily, Joan's aunt in Vaucouleurs was due to have a baby in the new year and somehow Joan persuaded her mum and dad it would be a good idea to send her to help, in spite of what happened last time. In January, Uncle Durand came to fetch her, and she left Domrémy once again. This time it would be for ever.

How to be a pain

Soon enough Joan found her way back to Captain Baudricourt. Unfortunately, the captain wasn't having a very good day. . .

Joan didn't buzz off, though. She stuck around. After her aunt's baby was born, she didn't go home but went back to Vaucouleurs and stayed for three weeks with a local wheelwright called Henry, and his wife Catherine.

Day after day Joan would go and visit the castle where the captain lived, and every time he went in or out she pestered him about taking her to the Dauphin.

Then, one evening Joan had a visit from two of Baudricourt's soldiers, called John and Bertrand. They'd seen the captain completely ignoring Joan and felt sorry for her. Compared with Baudricourt, these men seemed nice, and Joan was happy to talk to them:

> *I must be with the Dauphin before Easter, if I wear my legs down to my knees on the road. I would much rather be spinning by my mother's side . . . but I must do these things, because God wishes that I should do them.*

Impressed by Joan's simple words, John and Bert promised to try to help persuade the captain. Joan was beginning to get people on her side (hardened soldiers at that), and others soon followed.

Meanwhile, poor old Baudricourt was starting to lose a lot of sleep. . .

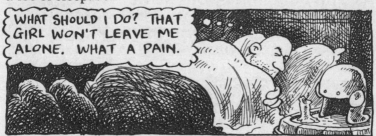

Vaucouleurs was a small place and the news about Joan had spread fast. People liked the idea of their little town being involved in God's plan to save France, and they were all in favour of helping Joan in any way they could. They'd also started to dub Joan 'the Maid' (meaning something like the 'Simple and Pure Unmarried Young Girl'), a nickname which would catch on fast.

Another thing that would catch on fast in *some* quarters was the idea that Joan was up to no good.

Excuse me, but are you a witch?

To be on the safe side, Baudricourt decided to take a priest to visit Joan at the wheelwright's house, to find out if she *was* a witch or a creature of the Devil or whatever. Unfortunately, the poor old priest didn't really know how to test for witches, and after a lot of umming and ahhing he just told Joan that if she was from the Devil she must keep away from him. So to 'prove' she wasn't a witch, Joan simply knelt down in front of the priest and asked for his blessing.

THAT'S GOOD ENOUGH FOR ME!

THIS IS RIDICULOUS!

Of course, even if she *had* been a witch she would have done exactly the same thing (unless she'd been a pretty stupid witch). Still, the test was enough for Baudricourt too, and he was now convinced she wasn't dangerous.

But he still didn't do anything.

Joan'll fix it (sort of)

There was nothing Joan could do but wait. She was restless, though, and often went to pray in the crypt of the church near Baudricourt's castle walls. There was a statue there of the Virgin Mary, and Joan knelt before it for hours at a time, praying intensely.

It wasn't long, however, before Joan had something more practical to occupy her. One day she received a strange invitation:

Duke of Lorraine's Ginormous House,
Nancy,
Not far away.

February 1429

Dear 'The Maid',

I am the Duke of Lorraine. You may have heard of me, I'm quite important round here. Anyway, I've heard of you... you're 'The Maid'. (Catchy name, I like it!)

Look, the thing is, I'm not very well. A little birdy told me that you get on famously with God. So can you fix it for me to be well again? Please come and see me so we can talk about it.

Your new friend,

The Duke of Lorraine

P.S. I've got bags of money, but you're probably not interested in that, being so holy and everything.

Joan was worried by the rumours now spreading about her. She didn't mind being called the Maid, and had even started to use the nickname herself, but the idea that she possessed healing powers was just mumbo-jumbo as far as she was concerned. The Duke was a very powerful man, though, and she couldn't just ignore him (even if he *was* a Burgundian). So she went to visit him and told him to his face that she didn't do miracles and that if he wanted to get well again he should live a better life and be nicer to his wife!

When Joan returned to Vaucouleurs, Baudricourt was still undecided about what he should do. Joan was so cross she went straight in to see him and said. . .

In God's name you are too slow; for this day near Orléans a great disaster has befallen our gentle Dauphin.

The captain didn't know what she was talking about. However, a couple of days later, there came news that the French army had been soundly beaten yet again in a big battle not far from Orléans.

The captain was now sure he had to do something. In any case, while Joan had been away, he'd written to the Dauphin, telling him all about her and it wasn't long before he got a reply, ordering him to send the Maid at once. To be honest, Baudricourt was quite happy to hand her over to the Dauphin and let *him* have the responsibility of deciding what to do with her.

As for Joan, she must have been delighted.

The new-look Joan

Charles's court was at a place called Chinon, 350 miles away, and the only way to get there was on horseback. It was going to be a very long and difficult journey, much of it through enemy country, so John and Bertrand decided Joan would need some new clothes. The simple red dress she usually wore wasn't very practical when it came to sneaking behind enemy lines and riding halfway across France. So they kitted her out in a sort of medieval equivalent of jeans, boots, and a thick woolly jumper. Joan's long black hair was cut short like a boy's, so that it wouldn't get in her eyes when she was riding.

BLACK CAP

SHORT HAIR

GREY TUNIC

BLACK DOUBLET

STURDY BOOTS

𝔐𝔈𝔇𝔌𝔈𝔙𝔄𝔏 𝔐𝔄𝔗𝔗𝔈ℜ𝔖

Women's clothes

Nowadays, women wear trousers and short hair all the time, but in the Middle Ages it was almost unheard of. A woman's place was at home, usually in the kitchen. They weren't supposed to go off riding horses, still less fighting battles. So people thought there was no need for them to dress like men. If they did, it was considered unnatural and *very* suspicious.

Eventually, Joan's tomboy look would get her into all sorts of trouble, but at the time it seemed like a good idea. She'd be able to pass much more easily through the countryside if people thought she was just an ordinary soldier.

JOAN'S SECRET DIARY (Aged 17)
Vaucouleurs, February 1429

Well, tomorrow I'll really be on my way at last. What a relief, after all this time.

Today I dictated a letter to be sent to my parents. Told them I love them very much, and said how sorry I am for deceiving them and running away. Explained to them I haven't any choice but to obey God. I just hope they understand.

As well as letting them know where I'm off to, I told them not to worry about me as I'm a grown-up girl now and I can look after myself. (Hmmm, not sure they'll see it that way!)

← MY NEW HAIR-DO

Joan's journey

Joan was to be escorted on her perilous journey by six men: her new friends John and Bertrand, two of their servants, a guard sent by the Dauphin himself, and just one other soldier. Captain Baudricourt himself was to stay at Vaucouleurs, and he must have been quite glad to see the back of Joan. Still, he wished her all the best. 'Go, and let come what may,' he told her.

With Joan in the lead, the little party left Vaucouleurs on a wet and rainy Sunday afternoon in February 1429. A small crowd waved goodbye, including Henry, Catherine and Uncle Durand.

The plan was to travel mostly by night and hide in the woods during the day when they would try to get a little sleep. There were enemy troops everywhere, and very few good roads. The rivers were in flood and lots of the bridges had been damaged or destroyed because of the war, so they were bound to get very wet. And it was still winter, of course, and very, very cold.

As the men in her party discussed the dangers ahead, Joan stayed calm and confident.

On the journey, which took eleven days, Joan saw for herself how many farms and villages had been razed to the ground by the English. She'd never been far outside Domrémy before, and probably hadn't realized just how much damage had been done. It must have made her even more determined to get to the Dauphin and help him free France from her enemies.

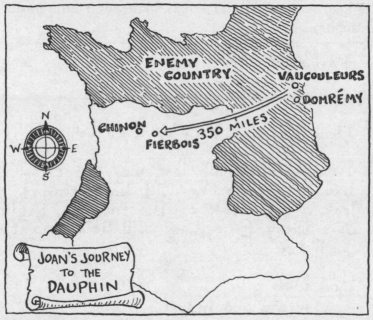

John, Bertrand and the others were amazed at Joan. To be honest, they hadn't been sure how she'd cope with such a difficult journey (what with her being a girl and everything). They weren't even sure she'd be able to ride properly over long distances. But Joan turned out to be a born rider and soon showed them how tough she really was.

Whenever they passed a church, Joan begged the others to stop so she could pray, and if possible take communion. But they were in enemy territory and John and Bertrand were afraid Joan would be spotted – news of the Maid had spread fast – so they only stopped twice.

At the church of St Catherine at Fierbois, Joan made sure she made up for lost time by taking communion three times in one day! (Perhaps it was because the church was dedicated to a saint who happened to be one of Joan's voices.) From Fierbois, Joan sent a letter to the Dauphin. . .

3rd March 1429

Dear Dauphin, Your Most Royal Highness,

I've come an awfully long way to see you, but I'm nearly there. I know things look a bit bleak at the moment, but don't worry. Everything will be all right, you'll see.

God bless.
Your friend and helper,
The Maid.

P.S. See you soon!

CHARLIE AND JOAN

Unlike Joan, no one at Chinon took the Dauphin Charles very seriously. He hung out with Armagnac nobles who claimed to support him, of course, but some of them bullied him and many laughed at him behind his back. Poor Charles was an awkward, ugly young man, who had trouble standing up for himself, and few of his nobles really believed he'd ever make much of a king.

In theory, Charles was supposed to be the most powerful man in France, but he wasn't very convincing. He was afraid of his own shadow and usually wore padded velvet

and furs from head to toe
because he was terrified
of catching a cold! He
was very superstitious
too, and was always
asking astrologers to read
his horoscope.

> I DON'T WANT TO HEAR ANYTHING BAD, THOUGH!

He didn't even have
all that much money and
often he had to borrow
it off of his own
nobles, which just made him seem even more weak and
feeble.

Although he was desperately unhappy about the awful
plight his country was in, Charles didn't know what to
do about it. He did like to call himself 'King of France'
now and then (when he was feeling big and brave), but
he still didn't dare get himself crowned properly. (The
English 'King of France', Henry VI, was still too young
to be officially crowned, so Charles had the chance to
get in there first.) Occasionally he would send his army to
fight the English here and there, but they never seemed
to have much luck. Mostly Charles just moped about at
Chinon, getting more and more depressed.

> YOU SEE, DAD WENT MAD AND MUM RAN OFF WITH MY WORST ENEMY, JOHN THE FEARLESS.

HE GOT KILLED AND MUM SAYS I MURDERED HIM. SHE SAYS I DON'T DESERVE TO BE KING.

THEN SHE PERSUADED DAD TO TAKE AWAY MY RIGHT TO BE KING JUST BEFORE HE DIED.

AND ON TOP OF EVERYTHING ELSE, EVERYONE LAUGHS AT ME BECAUSE OF THE WAY I LOOK!

STILL, IT'S GOOD TO KNOW I'VE GOT SOMEONE TO TALK TO.

All in all, it's not surprising that Charles pricked up his ears when he heard from Captain Baudricourt about a young girl who claimed to have been sent by God to help him. It must have sounded a bit strange, but Charles needed a friend (*any* sort of friend) more than anything else. He knew he was never going to become a proper king all by himself, and now he thought perhaps help was on the way. He must have been nervous though, because part of him was happy just to carry on living a quiet life, even if it did mean being a bit of a loser.

Among his nobles, opinion was divided. Most probably didn't believe Joan really *had* been sent by God. They just assumed she'd turn out to be a bit soft in the head, which would give everyone a good laugh. Still, some felt that the girl *might* help, even if she was a phoney. So long as Charles believed in her, that was all that mattered. What was there to lose? Others, however, had got so used to their cosy life at Chinon – with nothing to do but boss Charles about – that they didn't really want to be disturbed. Some of these tried to take advantage of Charles's superstitious nature and frighten him out of seeing Joan by telling him she might be a witch.

In the end, Charles overcame his fears and decided he *would* welcome Joan to his castle. (Actually, it was probably his mother-in-law who finally persuaded him!)

To be honest, almost everyone at court was curious about Joan, and Chinon must have been buzzing with excitement at the prospect of her arrival. Whatever they thought of her, most people probably couldn't wait to catch a glimpse of this upstart country girl.

Enter the Maid

Joan herself must have been really nervous as she began the long climb up to Charles's spooky-looking castle. The nobles who hung out with Charles were really rich and posh, even richer and posher than the Duke of

Lorraine, and they liked dressing up in all the latest fashions. To Joan, they must have looked pretty weird.

𝕸𝕰𝕯𝕴𝕰𝖁𝕬𝕷 𝕸𝕬𝕿𝕿𝕰𝕽𝕾

Fashions at court
Pointy shoes called 'poulaines' for the men and pointy 'steeple' hats for the ladies were especially popular.

SOME POULAINES EVEN HAD CHAINS TO HOLD THE POINTY BITS UP.

Poulaines became so pointy that at one stage laws had to be passed restricting their length!

And when Charles's mum Isabella moved into a new castle, she had to have all the doors made bigger to make room for her hat!

Still, Joan wasn't easily scared, and she kept her cool even as she was being ushered down the long corridors to the Great Hall where the king and his nobles were gathered.

Everyone was holding their breath when the doors finally opened and Joan stepped into the Great Hall. No doubt you could have heard a pin drop as Joan found herself surrounded by crowds of sniggering nobles with gawping faces. But again, she kept her head.

According to one story it was Charles who had a last-minute panic attack – he decided to hide! Just before Joan came in he leapt off his throne and ordered a servant to sit in his place while he mingled with his nobles.

The story goes that Joan wasn't fooled. She looked round for a moment and then walked right past the man who'd been told to sit on Charles's throne as a decoy. Instead she squeezed her way through the crowded room and approached Charles himself, who was cowering in a corner.

Gentle Prince, they call me Joan the Maid. The King of Heaven has sent me to you. . .

BUT HOW DID SHE KNOW IT WAS ME?

FACT OR FIB?

The angel with the golden crown

Joan later said that she'd seen an angel with a golden crown pointing to Charles.

But later still she admitted she was exaggerating, and that what she meant by an angel pointing was that somehow she *just knew* it was him. Joan had heard a lot about Charles by then, and it probably wouldn't have been difficult to spot him.

THAT'S HIM! THE FUNNY-LOOKING ONE WITH THE BIG NOSE!

Anyway, Charles was really impressed with this brave, confident girl. He took her aside to his private chapel and they prayed together. No one knows what Joan said to Charles in the chapel – she would never tell anyone – but whatever it was it went down a storm. When they came out Charles was beaming and everybody said he seemed to walk a bit taller. Perhaps she told him then and there about her voices and what they'd said. Whatever she said, she seemed to convey her enormous faith in him. That must have been a novelty for Charles and it perked him up no end.

Be my guest

Right away, Charles ordered the servants to prepare one of the towers of the castle for Joan to stay in, and gave her her own personal servant – a boy of about 12 called Louis – to help with her new life at court.

Every day Joan would go and talk to Charles and tell him what her voices were now urging her to do, i.e. get an army together to go and save Orléans. Then she was to go with Charles to the city of Rheims where he was to be crowned King of France. (All French kings were crowned at Rheims in those days.) She realized how important it was that he win the race to be a real grown-up king, properly crowned for everyone to see.

Unfortunately, Charles was soon having second thoughts. . .

Charles's Secret Diary

Chinon, March 1429

I don't know. All this fighting talk is a bit much for me. Joan seems like a very nice girl, but she's got some funny ideas, I must say.

My nobles tell me Orléans is as good as lost and there's no point trying to save it. And everyone knows Rheims is right in the middle of enemy territory. I don't fancy going there!

Besides, just think how wet and chilly it's going to be outside my comfy castle. I'll probably catch a nasty cold.

I think I'll just stay put for now. I mean, who wants to be king anyway? It sounds like far too much hard work to me. I'd much rather have a nice hot bath and go to bed early, thanks very much.

Joan got very frustrated. She would always love and respect her 'gentle Dauphin' (as she liked to call him) because of who he was – the future King of France. But now and then she must have got a tad impatient with him for being such a nervous nelly.

ARE YOU A MAN OR A MOUSE?

Charles's Secret Diary
Chinon, March 14-29

Hmmm, I wonder. Is Joan really from God? I thought so at first, but now I'm not so sure.

Lately I've heard even more sniggering than usual in the corridors of my castle. I think my nobles are laughing at me for believing in her. Is

So you're definitely not a witch then?

In the end, Charles thought he'd do what Captain Baudricourt had done and get Joan checked out by some religious experts. (That way he could avoid making any decisions himself.) So he sent her off to Poitiers, about 20 miles away, where there was a council of learned churchmen and theologians ready to ask her some tough questions.

SHOW US A SIGN THEN. OTHERWISE HOW CAN WE BELIEVE YOU'RE FROM GOD?

LOOK, I'M NO MAGICIAN, AND I DON'T DO MIRACLES, BUT IF YOU WANT A SIGN THEN GIVE ME AN ARMY TO TAKE TO ORLÉANS. IT IS GOD'S WILL THAT I SAVE ORLÉANS.

IF GOD IS GOING TO HELP YOU... THEN YOU WON'T ACTUALLY BE *NEEDING* ANY SOLDIERS, WILL YOU?

OOH, NICE ONE!

OH FOR GOODNESS' SAKE! THE SOLDIERS WILL FIGHT AND GOD WILL GIVE THEM VICTORY!

YOU TWIT!

JOAN'S SECRET DIARY

Poitiers, March 1429

What a day! Having to listen to all those silly old men banging on about this, that and the other. They spoke in ever such serious voices and said they represented 'the Church' as if it was God himself. Honestly, I love going to church, any church, but I'm not so keen on 'the Church'.

All those oh-so important churchmen - much too big for their boots - with all their posh clothes and clever-clogs arguments and book-learning...

Well, I've answered all their stupid questions, and now, it's up to them. I wonder what they'll decide to tell Charles.

MEDIEVAL MATTERS
Bishops, churchmen and the Church
There were no Catholics and Protestants in those days, just one single Church. Nevertheless, bishops and other churchmen often took different sides in wars. The churchmen at Poitiers were Armagnac supporters, but there were many who supported the other side. (The English and Burgundians offered them loads of money and power to keep them loyal.) They *all* claimed to represent the Church, though.

The churchmen at Poitiers didn't like Joan's bossy manner, and they weren't too keen on her men's clothes. They were also a bit put out by the idea that God was speaking to Joan in private. Normally when God spoke to men (or women) it was through the teaching of the Church. That's what the churchmen thought, anyway, because it made them feel important. But here was a girl who said she could have a chat with God any time she liked.

Still, they decided she definitely wasn't a witch and, like most people, they couldn't help being a bit impressed. In the end, after a lot of arguing, they reluctantly gave her the thumbs-up and told Charles she could be trusted. These days, Joan seemed to be able to convince *anybody* that she meant business.

Settling in

While Joan was away, Charles had moved his court to another town called Tours. (Perhaps he was hoping she wouldn't find him!) There, Joan soon began to settle in to life at court.

Some of Charles's nobles still mistrusted her, and weren't always nice, but many of the aristocratic women liked her. And she had her ever-faithful servant Louis, and John and Bertrand were there too.

In fact, before long Joan had a whole gang of people following her about whose job was to help her. She was given another servant called John, a personal weapons-trainer, and her very own priest so she could take communion as often as she liked! Joan must have felt very strange having all these people waiting on her hand and foot. It was never like this at Domrémy!

And news about Joan was spreading like wildfire. In the weeks since her first arrival at the Dauphin's court, Joan the Maid had become a legend all over France and as she walked about the town of Tours many people brought their children to her for a kiss and a blessing. Joan soon had to get used to being treated like a celebrity.

79

JOAN'S ARMY

Joan also made another new friend at court in the shape of a dashing young knight called the Duke d'Alençon.

D'Alençon had just returned from five years as a prisoner in England, but now his family had paid his ransom and he was keen to get back to the fight.

Armed with the facts

Ransoms

In medieval warfare, prisoners were often returned on payment of a ransom. The more important you were, the higher the price on your head. (The less important you were, the greater the chance that your enemies would kill you instead of bothering to keep you in prison!)

D'Alençon believed in Joan from the moment he met her and, because he was quite dishy, Joan always called him 'my handsome duke'.

It was d'Alençon who taught Joan how to fight. Each evening, after dinner, they'd go out to the fields and practise riding a horse and using a lance. For a beginner, Joan was amazingly good with a lance, and d'Alençon was so impressed he gave her a special present. It was a proper knight's warhorse. These were very expensive because they had to be specially trained and Joan was dead proud of it.

Suited and booted

Next she had a suit of armour specially made for her by the Dauphin's own armourer. He also knocked up a posh-looking armoured breastplate and other bits and pieces for her horse. She was being well and truly kitted out for war. No longer dressed as a mere boy, Joan now had all the gear you needed to be a knight in armour.

Medieval knights carried a lot of colourful flags and other paraphernalia so that they could be recognized in battle. Most knights carried the colours of their family's coat of arms, but since Joan's family weren't knights and had no coat of arms she had to choose her own. Her voices told her what to plump for:

WHITE SILK BANNER WITH GOLDEN LILIES, AND A PICTURE OF CHRIST BETWEEN TWO ANGELS HOLDING THE WORLD IN HIS HANDS.

LILIES — FLEUR-DE-LYS — WERE PART OF THE OLD ROYAL COAT OF ARMS, NOTHING TO DO WITH CHARLES BEING LILY-LIVERED!

PENNANT, THE ANGEL GABRIEL ANNOUNCES TO A GOBSMACKED VIRGIN MARY THAT SHE'S GOING TO BE A MUM.

JESU·maria

Finally, Joan had to get hold of a sword and again her voices helped by telling her where to find one. Joan sent a messenger to look behind the altar of the church at Fierbois. The messenger got the priest of the church to dig behind the altar and – lo and behold – they found a sword!

FACT OR FIB?

Joan's sword
Joan had stopped to pray to Saint Catherine at the church at Fierbois on her long journey from Domrémy to Chinon. Did she know that there was a sword there all along? Perhaps.

Joan's new rules

Joan was becoming more and more popular with the ordinary soldiers in the French army, who had also been readying themselves for war. The mood had changed among them since Joan's arrival. She'd had an amazing effect on them, making them a far more disciplined and organized lot than they were before. Medieval soldiers were a rough old bunch, and at first Joan must have been shocked by their behaviour. But she'd shown them the sharp side of her tongue and even managed to get lots of them to stop swearing!

JOAN'S SECRET DIARY

April 1429

It's great. Some of the men have even started going to Church! And they've all begun to drink a lot less and they spend less time chasing women. I've told them they should think of themselves as God's soldiers who should be on their best behaviour at all times. One of them told me he couldn't wait to charge into battle shouting, 'for God and the Maid'. That's the spirit!

Captain La Hire – whose nickname meant 'anger' – was a violent man, famous throughout the army for his colourful language and bad temper. But in Joan, he met his match.

There was something about La Hire that Joan liked, though, and he was fond of her too. But he found it impossible to stop swearing altogether and Joan had to agree to let him swear by his baton when the need arose. And when she asked him to say a prayer with her, he eventually came out with this: 'God: Please do for La

Hire what you would like La Hire to do for you if you were La Hire and La Hire were God.'

On the whole Joan got more respect from the ordinary soldiers than from the captains. Some of the knights gave her their support, like d'Alençon and La Hire. But others resented the way she was ordering them about. They wondered why they should listen to a teenaged peasant girl with a bee in her bonnet about voices from God. But even they had to admit she'd had a stunning effect on their men, and gradually they began to think it was worth putting up with Joan if it meant going to war with some chance of winning.

Charles was still hesitating, of course, afraid to send his newly perked-up army to fight for what seemed a lost cause at Orléans. But by now hardly anyone agreed with him, and he'd never been very good at standing up for himself. So it wasn't long before Joan's army was on the march.

MAID IN ORLÉANS

Only 60 miles from Paris, and looming above the wide River Loire that ran right through the middle of the country, the great city of Orléans was of vital military importance. Whoever controlled Orléans controlled the heart of France.

The English had been besieging Orléans for months, but they still hadn't captured it. They'd built a ring of wooden forts around the town, but hadn't yet built enough to cut it off completely and the French were still able to smuggle food and supplies through the gaps in the English lines.

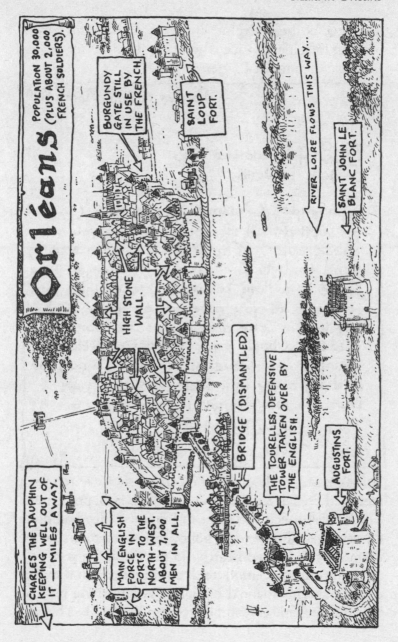

In charge of the besieging English army was the Earl of Suffolk. Imagine his face when he got this letter, which Joan had dictated at Poitiers:

Poitiers, 22nd March 1429

To Suffolk and the other English leaders,

Surrender Orléans to the Maid (ie. me), as well as all the other towns you've taken over. The Maid has been sent by God to help the King of France be king. She is willing to live in peace with you, so long as you give up, go home, and pay up for the damage you've done. So, please go back to your horrid little country and leave us alone. If not, me and my army will kick up such a fuss that you won't forget it in a hurry. Got it?

Yours sincerely,
The Maid (age 17)

Suffolk wasn't in the habit of receiving snotty letters from teenaged French females and he was soon hopping mad. The English ruled the roost in France – they had done for years – and now some gobby girl dared to challenge them? A girl! Who on earth did she think she was?

Unfortunately, Suffolk took out his anger on the poor young messenger who'd brought the letter! He put the boy in prison and threatened to burn him alive. This was against all the rules of war. You weren't supposed to put messengers – or heralds, as they were called – in prison, let alone kill them. (If heralds weren't free to travel safely between two sides in a war, how could enemies get in touch to say 'Truce!' or 'Stuff you!' or whatever?)

Whose army is it anyway?

Meanwhile, Joan wasn't paying much attention to the route her army was taking on its journey to Orléans. She'd left the navigating to d'Alençon and the other army captains. But eventually she noticed they were on the south bank of the Loire. That wasn't much good for attacking the main English forts on the north bank, which was what Joan had in mind. Suddenly she realized the other French captains didn't intend to attack the English right away, and they hadn't even told her. Not surprisingly, she was outraged.

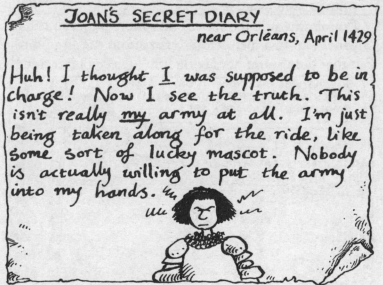

JOAN'S SECRET DIARY

near Orléans, April 1429

Huh! I thought I was supposed to be in charge! Now I see the truth. This isn't really my army at all. I'm just being taken along for the ride, like some sort of lucky mascot. Nobody is actually willing to put the army into my hands.

With Joan still seething, the French eventually reached the besieged city. They skirted round the English forts on the south bank and were met upriver by the man in charge at Orléans. He was Dunois, the son of Louis, Duke of Orléans (the one who'd been murdered by John the Fearless back in 1407).

It had been Dunois who'd ordered the army to arrive on the south of the river. His plan was to float cattle and fresh supplies across the river on barges. Unfortunately, though, because of a strong wind, the empty barges were stuck on the other side.

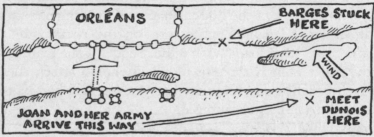

Dunois was an important duke – more important than anyone Joan had met before (apart from the Dauphin). But that didn't stop her giving him a piece of her mind!

PIFFLE! LET THEM WAIT UNTIL WE'VE BEATEN THE ENGLISH!

FLUTTER

YOU'LL NEED THEIR HELP AGAINST THE ENGLISH, BECAUSE EVEN YOUR ARMY ISN'T ENOUGH ON ITS OWN.

RUBBISH! JUST WAIT TILL I GET MY HANDS ON THEM...

FLOP

FLOP

FIRST WE MUST MAKE SURE THESE SUPPLIES GET INTO THE TOWN!

FLOP

DON'T YOU REALIZE GOD KNOWS BETTER THAN YOU DO! AND HE WANTS YOU TO LEAVE EVERYTHING TO ME!

FLUTTER!

FACT OR FIB?

The wind of change

Years later, Dunois said that, as he spoke with Joan, the winds gradually changed direction, allowing them to bring the barges across and load them up as planned. From that moment, he said, he believed in Joan.

It's quite possible that the winds did change while the French were discussing their plans, and perhaps Dunois did think it was some sort of miracle. But saying that Joan had 'miraculously' caused the winds to change might have been a clever way of getting her to agree to *his* idea!

Once the supplies were across, Dunois sent a large part of the army all the way back to the Dauphin to pick up yet *more* food and weapons.

Once again, Joan got cross. She thought she should be giving the orders, and she couldn't stand the idea of waiting around for this other stuff to turn up. As far as she was concerned it was high time to give the English the bashing they deserved, and the sooner the better.

However, she was just too tired to argue. (Being in a huff all day could be very wearing.) So she rested until it was dark, then crossed the Loire with Dunois and about 200 soldiers and entered Orléans. It was April 29th.

Three cheers for Joan!

When Joan got inside the town, she cheered up. The streets were all lit with blazing torches and there were people everywhere, shouting and singing her name! She was picked up and carried through the streets by the crowds. Everybody wanted to see her, and they all brought their children for her to bless. The people of Orléans had heard all about the Maid and, unlike the army captains, they trusted her completely – she was their saviour sent from God.

FACT OR FIB?

The blazing pennant

Joan's pennant was accidentally set alight by a passing torch. Some said Joan put the flames out with her bare hands, without flinching. A miracle?

Joan was very attached to her new pennant and perhaps she did burn her hands to save it. Or perhaps her gloves protected her hands.

The people of Orléans faced a terrible fate if the English took their city. They wanted to believe Joan had miraculous powers that might save them – and would probably seize any opportunity to 'see' Joan doing miraculous things.

That night Joan and her pages stayed with a local family (who must have been very excited to have had such an honoured guest). Joan took off her heavy armour, took communion, and had a small dinner. Then at last she slept.

A pointed message

The next morning, Joan got up early to have a look round the town while it was quiet.

JOAN'S SECRET DIARY

Orléans, Saturday 30th April 1429

What a lovely place. No _way_ am I going to let the English get their grubby mitts on it.

Got another message for them...

Dear English enemy,
Give me back my herald and
get lost. Yours sincerely,
The Maid.

Trouble is, I can't send another herald, or they'll keep him too. Must think of a better way to get my message across.

Later...

Tied my message to an arrow and fired it across! Simple. But the English just laughed. One of them shouted: 'Go back to your God damn farmyard, you silly cowgirl, or we'll burn you alive.'

I shouted back that he would die and go to hell sooner than he knew it. Then I burst into tears.

What idiot said 'Sticks and Stones will break my bones but names will never hurt me'? They deserve a punch on the nose! Oh well. Dunois says the English are just trying to wind me up.

First blood

A few days later, the rest of the army arrived with more supplies. Extra soldiers had been arriving from nearby cities, too, because the Dauphin had ordered every fighting man who could walk to come to Orléans.

Joan was excited, and it wasn't long before she saw some action. . .

JOAN'S SECRET DIARY
Orléans, 4th May 1429

I was taking a nap in my room when I was awoken by the noise of fighting. After all that hanging about, the battle had finally started without me!

Quick as I could I grabbed my armour, jumped on my horse, and headed for the battle. (I had to send my page Louis back for my banner, and he passed it through the window. Almost forgot it!)

When we got outside it was chaos. There were men running everywhere. I charged towards the Saint Loup fort, where the fighting was and planted my banner in the ground. But no sooner had I arrived than the English surrendered!

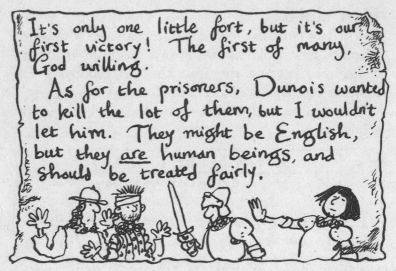

It's only one little fort, but it's our first victory! The first of many, God willing.

As for the prisoners, Dunois wanted to kill the lot of them, but I wouldn't let him. They might be English, but they <u>are</u> human beings, and should be treated fairly.

After her initial elation, Joan cried at the thought of the men who'd been killed in the fighting. For the first time she'd seen warfare up close and now realized what a bloody business it was. That day she went to confession with her priest and ordered all her men to do the same.

It turned out that the people of Orléans had got overexcited and attacked the English fort all by themselves. The captains, like Joan, had known nothing about it until they heard all the noise.

Tactics and tensions

The next day was Ascension Day. Joan announced that there wouldn't be any fighting on a holy day, and the captains went along with this. They didn't want to fight anyway because they *still* didn't think they were ready yet, but they kept quiet and just let Joan think she was in charge. Instead, the captains had a big Council of War meeting to discuss tactics behind Joan's back. Joan made do with sending another message to the English, telling them it was the last time she was going to bother writing and adding a PS asking them again what they'd done with her herald.

By now, the army was getting restless, and the captains knew they had to let the soldiers fight while they were in the mood. So the next day there *was* some serious fighting at Orléans, and Joan made sure she was right in the thick of the action. . .

ORLÉANS EVENING
HERALD
TOOT!

Friday 6th May 1429

DARING MAID WINS CRUCIAL VICTORY!

Thanks to the bold leadership of the Maid, the French army today moved a vital step closer to saving our lovely city.

This afternoon our brave boys (and our extra-brave girl) stormed across a makeshift bridge and attacked the St John-le-blanc fort, south of the river. Eyewitnesses report that the Maid herself was one of the first to get across. Straight away, she planted her banner and roared a challenge at the enemy.

At this, the English streamed out to attack. The handful of our lads who'd so far got across fought tooth and nail while the rest were still on the bridge.

Above the commotion, the Maid shouted encouragement on all sides, and eventually enough men were scrambled across to secure victory.

The Herald says: It was touch and go, but who cares! We won! Hurrah!

The people of Orléans went wild, of course, but the battle could easily have been a complete disaster. It was certainly brave of Joan to charge into the attack while most of the French army were still stuck on the island, but it wasn't very wise.

The French captains didn't know what to think. If it hadn't been for Joan there probably wouldn't have been any victory to celebrate. But they'd seen Joan put their army in terrible danger by being so headstrong, and she'd almost turned the whole operation into a complete fiasco. Should they trust her in future?

The captains told Joan they were sure it was 'by God's especial grace' that they had won their victory that day and Joan was really chuffed. But it may have been a polite way of saying they were lucky to be alive!

When they told her there was to be no more fighting until yet more reinforcements arrived, Joan went ballistic.

> *You have been to your council, and I to mine. And believe me the advice of my Lord will be put into effect, while your advice will perish.*

She meant that her voices knew better than any stupid army captains!

There were other voices on her side too, however, because the people of Orléans were crying out for more action. The captains soon realized that they'd *have* to fight the next day, because if they didn't the townspeople, led by Joan, would fight to the death without them.

Before Joan went to bed that night she told her priest to stay close by her in the fighting the next day. . .

> *For tomorrow the blood will spurt from my body above the breast.*

Joan's finest hour

Joan got up early on Saturday morning, before dawn, and took communion with her priest. Then she put on her armour and made her way through the town. Crowds of people wished her luck, while others begged her to lead them into battle. A passer-by offered her a fish for breakfast but Joan replied:

Keep it till supper tonight, for I will bring you a godam to have with it.

ᗔrmed with the facts

Godams

A godam was a name the French used for an Englishman, because all the English ever seemed to say was 'God damn'!

Joan led the townspeople across the river by boat, then did something even she hadn't dared to do before: she called her *own* Council of War meeting. She'd decided she was going to be giving the orders today. Seeing how many ordinary soldiers seemed prepared to listen to Joan, the captains decided to let her get on with it. If you can't beat Joan you might as well join her, they thought.

Here's what Joan planned to do. . .

ATTACK THE AUGUSTINS FORT AND FROM THERE ATTACK THE TOURELLES ITSELF.

TOURELLES

AUGUSTINS

At first the French made no headway at all, and the English in the Augustins fort started to jeer at them. Then, just as Joan was helping to prop up a scaling ladder, disaster struck. A crossbow bolt pierced Joan's armour and went right through her neck and shoulder till it was sticking out from both sides. It took a lot to shut Joan up, but that certainly did the trick, and she was quicky carried from the battle by some of her men.

When the bolt was torn out it must have been absolute agony – there wasn't any anaesthetic in those days, you simply had to grin and bear it. But Joan managed to shout a great cry of victory! Always one to look on the bright side, she took the fulfilment of the gloomy prophecy she'd made that morning as a fresh sign that God was with her.

FACT OR FIB?

Joan's prediction about her wound

Joan knew she'd be in the thick of the fighting and getting injured was always likely. However, Joan apparently predicted her wound several times, in front of witnesses, and also seemed to know she'd be wounded in the chest. One of these predictions is mentioned in a letter dated 22 April 1429, two weeks before she was injured!

Against all the odds, it wasn't long before she was up and about and back to her old self.

With Joan back on the field, the French kept up their attacks until evening, but still had no luck. Then, hoping for some advice from her voices, Joan left her standard with one of her men, and rode off to a quiet place near by to pray. While she was gone, though, the captains ordered the retreat.

When Joan returned and saw what was going on, she went berserk. Luckily, the man holding her standard had refused to budge without her say-so, and now she rushed forward and grabbed it off him. Despite her horrible wound, she waved her standard in the air and shouted at the top of her lungs.

This roused her men and they stormed into action once more. This time there was no stopping them and they quickly overwhelmed the fort that had given them such problems all day.

In the meantime, the people of Orléans had been busy using some old guttering and a few planks of wood to fill in the gap in the bridge leading to the Tourelles. They could now attack from the other side. The makeshift section of bridge was so low over the water that it was almost invisible and some French soldiers thought that people were actually walking on water! It all added to their growing belief that they were taking part in a miraculous victory.

There was now no way out for the English in the Tourelles, and they faced a horrible fate when the French set light to it. Some jumped in the river but were dragged under water by their heavy armour. The others gave themselves up and became prisoners. (Joan had got her godam, and more besides!)

Unfortunately, the battle for Orléans wasn't *quite* over. . .

ORLÉANS EVENING HERALD

TOOT!

Saturday 7th May 1429

VICTORY 'WITHIN OUR GRASP' SAYS MAID

The Marvellous Maid has led Orléans to an astonishing victory today. It may be only a matter of hours before the English surrender completely, she claims.

But others are more cautious. Although we're now kings of the castle in most of the forts on the south bank, the main English army is still a menace north of the river.

103

Nevertheless, by the following evening. . .

ORLÉANS EVENING HERALD

TOOT!

Sunday 8th May 1429

ORLÉANS FREE AT LAST!

Siege ends – English defeated for first time in yonks. Experts predict turning point in French fortunes.

Thanks to the miraculous Maid, we citizens of Orléans are finally free of the English pest! Three cheers for Joan!

After yesterday's stunning gains the city woke this morning to find the English gone from the remaining forts. Instead, they were gathered menacingly in the fields to the north of the city.

Wary of being lured into a battle on open ground, our captains were reluctant to take up the challenge.

The Maid gave another reason for holding back. 'It's Sunday,' she said. 'We shouldn't fight on a Sunday.'

When the English realized there was nothing doing, they decided to call it a day and rode off. Which means Orléans is finally safe.

The Herald says: At last! We've won a great victory! And all thanks to the Maid of Orléans! Three cheers for Joan!

FREE INSIDE! FULL-COLOUR MAID SUPPLEMENT TO CUT OUT AND KEEP!

Neither side could really quite believe what had happened but they knew one thing: it was Joan who'd made the French victory possible and she soon became known throughout France as the Maid of Orléans.

Inside the city, Joan could hardly move through the streets for people hugging her and kissing her and lifting her up on their shoulders and getting her to bless their babies. Not surprisingly, she loved it! She adored the city, and even found a house which she may have planned to live in when she'd finished giving the English their marching orders.

As it turned out, Joan never did get to live in Orléans, but years later her mum came to live there as a pensioner, and everyone treated her with the greatest respect. And every year, on the 8th May, the city has a big party in Joan's honour.

THE MARAUDING MAID

After Orléans, Joan went straight off to see the Dauphin. It was high time he was crowned properly and she was determined to get on with it. As for Charles, the news about Orléans had cheered him up no end, and he'd been busy writing to friends and acquaintances, telling them all about it.

Dear friends and acquaintances,

Guess what? My friend Joan has saved Orléans. It was easy-peasy pie, actually. So there. Nyah-nyah, nyah-_nyah_-nyah.

Charles of France.

PS So now you can all shut up about me being a loser.

When Joan arrived at Charles's court she wouldn't leave him in peace, but kept nagging at him and his top advisors to act now.

Gentle Dauphin, do not hold such long and wordy councils, but come to your coronation at Rheims. I am most eager that you should go there.

But Charles liked his council meetings, and the longer and wordier they were the better, as far as he was concerned. (After all, they didn't involve actually having to do anything.) In the end, though, he promised he *would* go to Rheims, but only after the army had won some more victories along the Loire to make the journey safer.

Joan agreed, and was pleased as Punch when Charles put her favourite duke, d'Alençon, in charge. She was full of confidence and promised his wife that she'd look after him, telling her that when he got back from this adventure he'd be in good health and probably in better shape than he was now!

BUT I LIKE HIM THIS SHAPE!

TUG

So, in early June 1429, Joan and d'Alençon set off with an army of about 2,000 men. In little more than a week they were to leave the English utterly humiliated.

Joan on the rampage

First to receive a visit from the Maid was a place called Jargeau. Joan shouted her challenge as usual, but instead of shouting back rude words as they had at Orléans, this time the English were completely silent. They were frightened of Joan now, and didn't dare mouth off.

Joan threw herself into the battle with all her usual gusto. . .

. . .and even managed to save d'Alençon's life.

(Well she had promised his wife she'd look after him!)

In the end, the town was taken, but not before 1,100 Englishmen had been killed in the fighting.

The French returned to Orléans for a rest, but Joan was soon urging d'Alençon (who was supposed to be the one in charge!) that she expected the army to be ready for action very soon. A few days later the French took the town of Meung. Two days after that, Joan and her handsome duke booted the English out of yet another town, this time a place called Beaugency.

An ugly scene

Then, on 18th June 1429, the French won the Battle of Patay, one of the grizzliest in the Hundred Years War, and one that many saw as revenge for the slaughter at Agincourt 14 years before. Here's what seems to have happened:

The French said Joan was responsible for the victory, but in fact she only arrived on the scene after most of the killing had already been done. La Hire's soldiers had been merciless, and though Joan was delighted by the victory, she was horrified by what she saw. According to some reports, over *two thousand* English soldiers had been butchered as against only *three* French casualties.

Joan saw one French soldier smash a captive Englishman over the head with his sword, and as the Englishman lay dying Joan nursed him in her lap and begged him to make his confession. Then she sobbed as he died in her arms.

110

Joan had always been up for a fight. And although she later claimed that she never actually killed anyone herself, she seemed to enjoy wearing her armour, raising her standard, and charging off into battle for the French cause. But when she saw what her army had done at Patay, she must have wondered what she was doing urging her men to commit mass murder like this. It must have turned her stomach to think that her own actions had led to such suffering.

Points of view

Among the French, there wasn't a man who didn't now believe in Joan's power to help them, and many believed she herself was helped by God. Now the English also began to believe in her – it's just *what* they believed that was different. Here's how they reasoned:

It might seem silly, but people were a lot more superstitious in those days, and many English soldiers probably did believe Joan really was a witch. But even those who weren't so gullible, like the more educated nobles and captains, still went round *saying* Joan was a witch. At least it gave them some sort of excuse for their poor performance on the battlefield. And one day it would give them an excuse to shut Joan up for good.

CORONATION CHICKEN

Joan had now proved that her great victory at Orléans was no fluke. She hadn't kicked the English out of France altogether, but she'd got them on the run. And the French army had been transformed from a hopeless bunch of losers into a top-notch fighting force. Thousands of men from all over France now rushed to join up and get a piece of the action. (This wasn't *all* good news for Charles, who wasn't sure how he was going to pay everybody!)

Although the army was now all for pressing on and bashing the enemy at Paris, Joan's number one priority was to get Charles crowned at Rheims so there'd be no more arguments about who was the true King of France.

Rheims was still well inside Burgundian territory, though, and going there would be dangerous, so Charles *still* wasn't sure he wanted to be crowned just now, thank you very much. Joan had to work as hard as ever to convince him it was a good idea.

To get the coronation firmly on the agenda, Joan got cracking with some invitations:

25th June 1429

To The Citizens of Tournai

PLEASE COME TO A PARTY!

You are invited to join me, Joan, the Maid of Orléans, for a big party at Rheims to celebrate the coronation of King Charles of France! Please bring all the family and help to make this a really special occasion.

PS Why not bring a friend (or two)?

PPS The more the merrier.

In the end she managed to persuade Charles. . .

OH, I SUPPOSE YOU KNOW WHAT YOU'RE DOING...

. . .and on 29th June 1429, they finally set off. Joan must have been very proud. Even though Charles was a pain sometimes, it still must have given her a huge thrill to be actually riding alongside her gentle Dauphin, up at the head of her all-conquering army.

In fact, it was going to be a long journey that would take several days. And they had to pass through lots of towns that were still in enemy hands. Although Charles was worried sick about this, Joan was sure they'd surrender when they saw the Maid coming. She was used to getting her way by now.

But it wasn't quite as easy as Joan thought because the first town they came to, Auxerre, refused to open its gates. Joan thought it would have been a piece of cake to attack the town, but Charles and his nobles preferred to avoid a fight if they possibly could and bribed their way in instead.

Joan was furious when they weren't allowed into the next town, either, which was Troyes (of treacherous treaty fame). A measly 500 enemy soldiers kept the gates closed, but once again Charles wouldn't let swords be drawn. So the French army camped outside the city while the two sides tried to strike a deal.

Brother Richard

It was while she was kicking her heels outside Troyes, that Joan made a new acquaintance. One day she saw a friar (a type of monk) tiptoeing towards her nervously. . .

115

Brother Richard was quite a celebrity in France, and had made a name for himself after preaching to huge crowds in Paris, telling them that the end of the world was nigh and that they should get rid of their possessions and become more holy.

Richard had heard all about Joan, of course, and when she arrived at Troyes, where he was staying, he wanted to meet her for himself. He was wary, though (like so many before him), and was worried at first that she might be a witch.

Once they got chatting, however, Joan soon persuaded him she was wasn't going to turn him into a toad, and before long they'd become friends. Joan even persuaded Richard to swap sides. Until now he'd supported the English and the Burgundians, but after meeting Joan he threw in his lot with Charles.

Unfortunately, hanging out with Richard didn't do Joan any favours really, and only got her into trouble. Many high-up people in the Church thought Richard was a rabble-rouser, whose radical ideas might encourage people to revolt against them.

Now they saw Joan in the same light, as someone who was actively encouraging people to oppose the Church itself.

To make matters worse, Richard egged Joan on to speak much more openly about her voices than she'd ever done before. (The voices that the bishops who'd questioned Joan at Poitiers had been so suspicious about.) And he also went round telling stories about her having special powers, even claiming she could make the French army fly if she wanted! But this only encouraged rumours that she really was a witch.

Joan gets busy

Even with Brother Richard around to keep her entertained, Joan couldn't stand all this hanging about and soon decided it was time for action...

117

1 First, she told the Dauphin that if he'd just put her in charge she'd have them inside Troyes before he could say, 'Are you sure that's a good idea?' Then she started dishing out orders.

2 Next she sketched a complex plan of attack which impressed the captains while she informed the men of the basic idea.

3 Then she raced ahead to give the signal for the attack to begin. In fact, the town surrendered straight away. They knew they couldn't hold out for long against a full-scale attack from the Mighty Maid.

4 Then she burst into Troyes and got busy organizing a big reception for Charles, lining her soldiers along the streets to give him a rousing welcome.

5 Next she popped in to visit a baby who'd just been born, and whose mum had asked Joan to bless it and be its godmother!

6 Then she hightailed it back to join Charles himself as he rode into town in a stately procession.

7 Finally, she plonked herself down and had a breather. As usual, being the Maid was all go.

FACT OR FIB?

The butterflies

An eyewitness at Troyes reported seeing a cloud of butterflies swirling around Joan's banner.

Joan's banner was white, with golden lilies dotted all over it. Could they have been mistaken for butterflies?

Luckily for Joan the next town they came to, Châlons, opened up straight away. Châlons wasn't all that far from Lorraine and here Joan had a nice surprise. . .

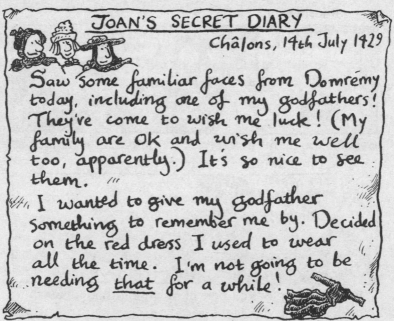

JOAN'S SECRET DIARY

Châlons, 14th July 1429

Saw some familiar faces from Domrémy today, including one of my godfathers! They've come to wish me luck! (My family are OK and wish me well too, apparently.) It's so nice to see them.

I wanted to give my godfather something to remember me by. Decided on the red dress I used to wear all the time. I'm not going to be needing <u>that</u> for a while!

Knock, knock

The next day, though, Joan was anxious. Even though Rheims was only about a day's march away, she suddenly became worried that something might go wrong and mess up her plans. There were still quite a few enemy troops in the city, and the main English and Burgundian armies weren't far away either. Joan still couldn't be sure that the people of Rheims itself would actually agree to the coronation.

In fact, Charles had already written to them:

> ## Dear People of Rheims,
>
> Sorry to bother you, but is there any chance you could let me in so I can get crowned properly? I promise I won't be any trouble. I just need to use the cathedral for a few hours.
>
> Yours sincerely,
> Charles, your rightful ruler. (No offence.)

The people of Rheims thought about it for a bit, but finally agreed to open the gates. So, on Saturday 16th July 1429, Charles, Joan, and the French army marched into Rheims, while the Burgundian troops marched out through a different gate. (They'd realized the town was all in favour of a coronation party and they thought it best to make a quiet exit.)

Once inside, Joan decided there was no point in hanging about in case more enemy troops turned up and spoiled the whole thing so she fixed the date of the coronation for the very next day. That only gave them a few hours to get ready!

A bit of a do

If you ever find yourself having to organize a French medieval coronation at very short notice, here's what you need:

- Tonnes of fancy royal regalia to use as decorations (banners, flags and whatnot to give a bit of colour).
- Twelve Peers of the Realm. (The 12 poshest bishops and nobles in France.)

- Rheims cathedral. (You can't just use any old one: it has to be Rheims.)
- A bottle of very special ancient holy oil to anoint the new king with.
- Crowds of screaming fans.

Though she was sorted for the oil, the cathedral and the fans, Joan only had three of the proper bishops (but no other Peers of the Realm) and none of the fancy royal stuff. True to form, she made do with what was available. . .

Peers of the Realm were thin on the ground that day because several of them now supported Charles's enemies. They thought the English king, Henry, was the real King of France, not Charles – so there was no way they'd be turning up for *this* coronation. (One such peer was Philip the Good, the Duke of Burgundy, because technically he was just an important French noble, not a ruler in his own right. Joan must have known he wouldn't come, but that hadn't stopped her from sending him a cheeky invite a few weeks before!)

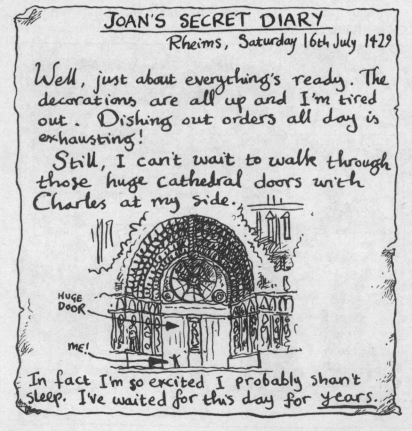

JOAN'S SECRET DIARY
Rheims, Saturday 16th July 1429

Well, just about everything's ready. The decorations are all up and I'm tired out. Dishing out orders all day is exhausting!

Still, I can't wait to walk through those huge cathedral doors with Charles at my side.

HUGE DOOR →

ME!

In fact I'm so excited I probably shan't sleep. I've waited for this day for <u>years</u>.

Joan's big day lived up to all expectations and ended up being probably the happiest day of her life. Here's how it went. . .

THE GALLIC GLOBE

17th July 1429

FRANCE SALUTES KING CHARLES VII!

Proud Maid sees beloved Dauphin crowned at last.

France's true king, Charles VII, has at last been anointed and crowned at Rheims cathedral. In an emotional service, the Dauphin today claimed his right to be called King and in hushed tones swore an oath 'to protect the people of France from all injustice' (i.e. the English).

The Maid of Orléans stood by her beloved Charles throughout. Unusually, she was even allowed to hold up her banner inside the cathedral. 'It fought the battles, so it should get the glory,' she later commented.

When the ceremony was over a loud trumpet-burst signalled that now it was time to celebrate – and how!

The Maid, here seen with Captain La Hire and the Duke d'Alençon, afterwards described herself as 'over the moon' now that the long-awaited coronation had come off so successfully.

'I always knew Charles could do it,' she said. 'He just needed a bit of encouragement, that's all.'

When the service was over, Joan went with Charles and all the other nobles to the coronation banquet, which must have been quite a party.

After that, Charles couldn't wait to show off his new crown, so Joan went with him to ride around the town and let everybody gawp at him in all his finery. The crowds were huge – and of course everybody seemed to have at least one baby for her to bless!

JOAN'S SECRET DIARY
Rheims, Sunday 17th July 1429

Guess who I saw in the crowd, today? Dad! and Uncle Durand too! I couldn't believe it!

They both had tears in their eyes. It was so good to see them again – I burst into tears myself and leapt off my horse to give them a big hug. Dad is staying in an inn called the Striped Donkey, opposite the cathedral. He looks tired, but he says he's proud of me.

Later, Charles asked me if there was anything he could give me to say thanks for making him king. Normally I would have said no — I mean, I'm not doing all this for a reward. But there <u>was</u> something that occurred to me. I asked if he'd let off the people of Domrémy from paying taxes from now on. Poor old Charles. He looked gutted when I said that. I know he's a bit short of cash himself. Still, in the end, he agreed. Bless him, he's such a sweetie!

What Joan never realized, though, was that Charles wasn't a sweetie at all, and it wouldn't be long before he let her down terribly. . .

THINGS GO WRONG

As far as Joan was concerned, next stop was Paris. She was in high spirits, and thought her army would soon take the city, even though it was well-defended by English and Burgundian troops. From Rheims, she'd already written one of her stinging letters to the Duke of Burgundy, Philip the Good, telling him to sling his hook. France now had her king, she told him, and through him God would soon punish her enemies. (She also ticked him off for not coming to the coronation!) It was the usual tough talk, but things soon started to go wrong for Joan.

The thing was, Charles had different ideas. Fighting a war was expensive, and Charles was worried about how he was going to pay his army. Some of his men had started to complain about not having enough to eat. Besides, Charles began to think that even with Joan's help he could never win a war against two enemies (England *and* Burgundy).

So, behind Joan's back, he also wrote to Philip the Good. . .

August 1429

Dear Phil,

As you may have heard, I am now the King of France. But don't worry, I'm not really looking for a fight. It's such a messy business. And dangerous, too.

I thought perhaps we might come to an arrangement. Tell you what: if you promise to stop teaming up with the English, I'll let you keep some nice bits of France.

Don't worry about Joan. She gets a bit overexcited. She's a smashing girl, she really is, but a bit too bossy for my liking. I think it's time I did things <u>my way</u> - i.e. sneakily.

Your new friend,

Charlie

PS It wasn't my idea to murder your dad. Honest!

Charles rode with the army on the march towards Paris, but he was dragging his heels more than ever and hoping to tie up a deal with Burgundy before he got there.

Some miffed bishops

On the way, several more enemy-held towns surrendered, including Senlis, Beauvais, and Compiègne. But, at each of these places, something happened that would one day make trouble for Joan. . .

1 At Beauvais the town's pro-English bishop – Pierre Cauchon – was forced to run away to Paris, losing his nice comfy home. He wouldn't forget this humiliation in a hurry.

2 At Compiègne Joan was just mounting her horse, impatient to get on with the day's fighting, when she was interrupted by a messenger. . .

₥ЄⅅłЄVⱭℒ ₥ⱭƫƫЄℛ₷

Two Popes?

The Pope is the head of the Catholic Church. He is supposed to be God's spokesman on earth, so obviously there's only meant to be one of him at a time. But from 1378–1417 there'd actually been two rival popes. (And, at one point, three!) One lived in Rome (Italy) and one in Avignon (France). Even after 1417, deciding which had been the real one was still one of the hottest political issues of the day.

It might not seem much, but Joan's casual reply annoyed some people. Important bishops and churchmen had been sounding off for *years* about this question, but Joan seemed to think she could just get a direct answer from God without listening to what they had to say at all.

3 At Senlis, Joan was accused of stealing! Impatient to be getting on for Paris, she'd found herself temporarily horseless. So, without asking, she borrowed the extremely expensive horse belonging to the town's bishop. She'd got used to people willingly lending her anything she needed, but now she was taking liberties. . .

Dear Bish,
Borrowed your
gee-gee.

Ta.

Joan.

Worse still, when Joan heard the bishop was angry she sent it back with a note that said. . .

Dear Bish,
Here you are.
It's a rubbish
horse, anyway.
Joan.

High walls and secret deals

The French army reached the outskirts of Paris on 26th August 1429. They quickly dug down outside, while their enemies organized their defences around the huge old city walls.

In those days Paris was the biggest city in Europe, with a population of 100,000. France's enemies had taken it over some years before, when Charles had run for his life and thousands of Armagnacs had been massacred. Now, most Parisians backed the 3,000 English and Burgundian soldiers who defended the city.

Paris was always going to be a tough nut for Joan to crack, but as usual she refused to think about the difficulties. After Orléans, anything was possible, and even though she hadn't heard much from her voices lately, Joan was sure God would help her.

What she didn't realize was that her own king wasn't really on her side any more. While she and d'Alençon made preparations for what promised to be the biggest battle of them all, Charles was still making secret deals. . .

August 1429

Dear Phil,

Look, I'm not really interested in having a fight. I've got what I want, a nice shiny crown and really quite a big bit of my country.

Let's have a truce. That way I can get away from these nasty battles and go back to my comfy castle.

Don't worry about Paris. There's no way I want to see my army smashed to smithereens just for a measly capital city, even if it *is* the finest in Christendom.

Your new friend,

Charlie

PS The trouble is, all those victories (no offence) have gone to Joan's head! Anyway, let's just let her fight for a day or two and she'll soon realize she's out of luck.

Maid meets moat

For a couple of weeks, nothing much happened. But Joan soon got fed up with all the shilly-shallying and finally ordered the attack on Paris to begin on 8th September, even though her voices hadn't told her to do so. Strangely, the day she chose was a special Holy Day in honour of the Virgin Mary. At Orléans, Joan hadn't wanted to fight on a holy day – and not even on a regular Sunday – because she was afraid God would be angry, but now she didn't seem to think twice about attacking Paris on one of the holiest days of the year.

As it turned out, the attack on Paris was a complete and utter disaster. This is what happened. . .

SHE ORDERED HER MEN TO PUSH WAGONS FULL OF
LOGS AND STONES INTO THE MOAT TO MAKE A
BRIDGE... BUT THEY SANK WITHOUT TRACE. THIS MOAT
WAS MUCH DEEPER THAN ANY SHE HAD COME UP AGAINST
BEFORE...

AN ENGLISH CROSSBOWMAN LAUGHED AT HER, CALLED
HER RUDE NAMES, AND SHOT HER THROUGH THE THIGH
WITH ONE OF HIS BOLTS.

JOAN'S STANDARD BEARER WAS SHOT IN THE FOOT A
MOMENT LATER. HE LIFTED HIS VISOR TO EXAMINE
THE WOUND AND WAS INSTANTLY SHOT A SECOND
TIME, THIS TIME IN THE FACE.

The next day the King actually ordered Joan and her army to give up and turn back from Paris altogether. Joan was upset and angry, but she was also badly wounded and had no choice but to obey.

The French soldiers were shocked and frightened. They didn't know what to think now. They'd begun to believe everything was going to be easy with Joan on their side, but now everyone could see that she was no miracle-worker. She couldn't *always* lead them to victory. The battle for Paris, Joan's first defeat, was a real turning point in her story. From now on things would go from bad to worse . . . until they got really, really awful.

THINGS GET WORSE

After the fiasco at Paris, Joan began to feel very down in the dumps and much of her confidence seemed to drain away. Her voices had guided her to some great victories, and to Charles's coronation at Rheims, but they hadn't told her to attack Paris that day, and when she had, it had been a disaster. Had she got carried away? As she rested her injured leg she thought about all this and got more and more depressed. In fact, she'd never again be quite her old self.

Joan, VIP

Despite recent setbacks, however, Joan was as popular as ever with many ordinary people, who continued to treat her like a celebrity. They called her things like the 'Angelic One', and hung pictures of her all over the

137

place. And, of course, they still got her to bless babies left, right and centre.

There wasn't much Joan could do about people turning her into a superstar, but it got her into trouble later. Her enemies resented her popularity and thought it gave her ideas above her station.

Unfortunately for Joan, Charles was also fed up with her VIP status – he didn't like people thinking she was more important than him! Besides, Charles felt he no longer had much use for a Maid meddling in his affairs and telling him what to do all the time. He was at peace with Burgundy now, and these days the English were less of a threat (thanks to Joan's victories, of course!) so he didn't think he needed her help any more. And of course Paris had proved that even Joan couldn't *guarantee* victory, so Charles now started to treat her like a lucky mascot that had ceased to be lucky.

Like many people, Joan didn't think the truce with Philip the Good – who was a slime-ball, as everyone knew – would last. (Peace would only be won 'at the point of a lance', she liked to say.)

Not surprisingly, then, she was soon making plans to join up with d'Alençon and attack the English again, but the King wouldn't let her go. He more or less banned Joan from fighting, and he wouldn't even let her *see* her 'handsome duke'. (In fact, after Paris, Joan was never to see him again.) After all she'd done, Joan now found herself grounded.

AND THERE ISN'T EVEN ANYTHING ON TELLY FOR ANOTHER FIVE HUNDRED YEARS!

POIK

Joan meets a rival

Without any fighting to do, Joan was soon bored. But things livened up when she was introduced to a friend of Brother Richard's called Catherine de la Rochelle, a woman who claimed to see visions. Joan was excited to meet someone with experiences similar to her own and she told Catherine all about her voices and what they'd said to her over the last few years. Then she asked Catherine about her visions.

Catherine explained that at night she often saw a beautiful white lady, dressed in gold, who told her to travel through the towns and villages collecting gold and silver to pay for the King's army. This ghostly lady would tell Catherine if anyone was hiding any gold or silver from her.

For some reason, though, Joan didn't think Catherine's story rang true. (Perhaps because the lady sounded more like a ghost than a vision.) In fact, Joan didn't believe it at all. . .

JOAN'S SECRET DIARY
November 1429

I told Catherine to stop pretending to be a visionary like me. 'You ought to go back to your husband,' I said, 'and get on with some housework instead!'

White ladies! Whatever next?

Just to be sure, I asked my voices whether to believe Catherine. They said no, Catherine was 'but folly and all nothing'. Well, that's exactly what I thought. So I wrote to Charles telling him not to trust her.

Later, at Christmas, Joan must have had second thoughts. She asked if she could sleep in the same bed as Catherine and see if she could catch a glimpse of the woman in white herself!

JOAN'S SECRET DIARY

FIRST NIGHT

Stayed up all night but the White Lady didn't show up (surprise surprise).

SECOND NIGHT

I was so tired after staying up last night that I fell asleep straight away. In the morning Catherine said the White Lady had visited while I was snoozing. (Oh yeah, I bet she did!)

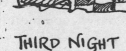

WOOOO!

ZZZZ

THIRD NIGHT

Kept myself (and Catherine) awake all night by talking non-stop. For example, kept asking Catherine when exactly we could expect a visit from You Know Who. She kept saying 'Soon, soon', but it was another no show.

Let's face it, Catherine, <u>the White Lady is piffle</u>.

It seems that Joan didn't like having a rival visionary knocking around, claiming to get messages from God just like her! But it was a bit unfair to insist on seeing Catherine's lady. After all, Joan wasn't all that keen on showing other people evidence of *her* voices and visions. When her servant John once asked if he could see them she told him he wasn't holy enough!

Joan's invisible army

As the winter dragged on, Charles knew Joan was getting bored and frustrated so as a special treat he let her fight one more battle for him. A town called La Charité was held by a French noble who'd thrown in his lot with the English, and Charles thought he could send Joan to sort him out without endangering his delicate peace talks with Philip the Good. Naturally, Joan was up for it, and for a while it looked like she might be back to her old self.

Then, during some fierce fighting near La Charité, Joan found herself in a tight corner, along with just five other French soldiers. They were completely outnumbered by the enemy, and about to be cut off, so Joan's servant, John, rushed up and urged her to run. Joan shouted back. . .

I am not alone. There are fifty thousand men in my company.

Somehow she and her men fought their way out of this very sticky situation and everyone called it the Victory of the Angels because of Joan's army of fifty thousand invisible soldiers. Some people thought the angels were real which showed that Joan was back on top form, with God clearly on her side. But others thought she must have been delirious, which only showed that she was cracking up.

The next day the French got badly battered, and with or without her army of angels, Joan didn't manage to capture La Charité. In fact, it was another serious defeat, and Charles now preferred to keep his not-so-mighty Maid indoors and out of harm's way.

Arise, Sir and Lady Darc

At Christmas, Charles decided to cheer Joan up by making her whole family into nobles. That meant her dad and brothers were now honorary knights and could wear Joan's coat of arms with the *fleur-de-lys* on it.

Unfortunately, Charles didn't give them any land or money to go with their new title, because he was completely flat broke. (Charles was now so poor he had to pawn his own crown jewels. And in one town he visited, a cobbler even had the cheek to refuse to make him some shoes because he didn't believe the King would pay up!)

Yours crossly

Joan was still bored at court, but she kept herself busy in the new year by writing some letters. . .

1 First, she dashed off a quick note to a town called Tours, asking the treasurer there for a special favour (i.e. telling him what to do). The daughter of the Scottish artist who'd painted her standard was getting married in Tours and Joan wanted to make sure the town gave her some money for a nice wedding!

2 Then Joan dropped a line to some religious-types in Bohemia (in eastern Europe) called the Hussites. They thought the Church was too rich and wanted to worship God in their own way, without kowtowing to what know-all bishops said all the time. Joan might have sympathized with the Hussites if she'd known them better. But they lived a long way away in another country and she'd heard only that they were causing trouble for their ruler, the Holy Roman Emperor. Charles was trying to make friends with him, so Joan thought she'd help him with her letter.

Actually, this letter was written in Latin (a language that all educated people in Europe understood and which was often used for important international letters). Joan didn't understand Latin, so she probably just suggested the ideas for this letter, whilst someone else wrote it. Anyway, this is roughly what it said:

23rd March 1430

Dear Hussites,

Please stop being Hussites, right this minute, and behave yourselves. Otherwise I might just come and visit, <u>with my army.</u> (If I hadn't been so busy I'd have done it already.)

Yours sincerely,
The Maid.

3 Joan also wrote twice to Rheims, encouraging the people there to continue supporting Charles and telling them not to be afraid of the enemy. 'I will make them fasten their spurs so fast that they will not know how to put them on and get out of there, and very quickly at that,' she wrote. Joan's sentences didn't always make perfect sense, but everyone knew what she meant! This was a strong hint that she'd soon be back in the fray.

Going it alone

It'd now been months since Joan had seen any action, and she was fed up. So, as usual, she decided to take matters into her own hands. If Charles didn't want her help, and wouldn't let her near his army or his other captains, then she'd just have to do her best without them. She hadn't heard much from her voices recently, but instead of waiting around for them, she decided to act on her own.

So one day she told everyone at court that she was popping out for some air. Then she took her servant John and a few others with her, and rode off looking for a fight.

Before long, she'd joined up with a small army of soldiers. Many of these men were probably mercenaries – professional soldiers who would fight for anybody who would pay them – and therefore not easily controlled by Charles, who could hardly pay for his own dinner. (The mercenaries were probably being paid by rich French nobles who wanted to fight for control of individual towns here and there.)

Once, with the King's backing, Joan had ridden into battle at the head of the whole French army – as many as 12,000 men at one point.

Now she'd gone behind the King's back and joined a motley crew of just three or four hundred rough and ready men.

Bad behaviour

It may have been at this time that Joan discovered her soldiers had smuggled some women into their camp for a bit of fun. Joan had already made it clear to her men that snogging girls was strictly not allowed in her army, and her reaction was typical:

It was said that Joan smashed her sword, the one she'd miraculously discovered in the church at Fierbois. When Charles eventually heard about this he got quite upset and told Joan she shouldn't have used her special sword 'upon so unworthy an object' as a girl's bottom. He told her she should have used a stick instead! Even at the time, some people thought the smashed sword was a very bad sign.

There were soon more serious signs that all was not well. . .

Lagny, April 1430

Dear Duke d'Alençon,

I hope you don't mind me writing to you, but I'm worried about Joan. She doesn't seem herself at all.

The other day we surprised a group of Burgundian soldiers here in Lagny. It wasn't pretty, and there was a lot of blood. We also took some prisoners, including the Burgundian captain. Joan promised him he would live and told him she wanted to swap him for a French prisoner that the Burgundians had got.

But later, when Joan found out that the Frenchman had died in prison, she ordered <u>our</u> prisoner to be handed over to a nearby town for trial, knowing full well that he'd be found guilty and executed. (Which he was.)

I know Joan's really miserable, but it's not like her to be so heartless. She'd <u>promised</u> the man he'd live.

Your worried friend and servant,

John (servant to the Maid)

Joan even stole the man's sword, to replace the one she'd broken so unluckily, and boasted that it was...

... good for swiping and slashing.

Joan's whole attitude to fighting seemed to have changed, and she was behaving more ruthlessly than before. Had she let the bloodthirstiness of her warmongering mercenaries rub off on her? The whole episode certainly shows that Joan was no angel, whatever people might call her.

FACT OR FIB?

The baby at Lagny

At Lagny, Joan was asked to pray for a baby that had died. She was told that the baby hadn't moved for three days and Joan said it was 'as black as my cloak' when she first saw it. Before long, though, it yawned three times. It did die shortly afterwards, though, but its parents just had time to baptize it properly. (A baby that hadn't been baptized couldn't be buried in holy ground, i.e. a churchyard.)

Bad news

One evening in April 1430, Joan was sitting in a ditch, watching her men round up the last of the enemy soldiers after another minor skirmish, when she heard her voices again. . .

This time, though, what they told her must have chilled her blood. They said that before the Feast of St John (24th June), which was two months away, Joan would be captured by the enemy. They told her not to be scared, and to have faith because God was with her. Joan *was* scared, though, and even prayed that she might die rather than be captured.

CAUGHT!

In spite of what her voices had told her, Joan didn't lose her hunger for action. A few weeks later, with a whole month to go before the Feast of St John, Joan rode right through the night to get to another battle on time. It would be her last.

Charles's truce with Philip the Good was now in tatters. (As Joan and others had predicted, Philip hadn't stuck to his side of the bargain.) So Charles was now happy to have Joan fighting for him again, and gave her his backing.

SHE HAS HER USES, I SUPPOSE.

The town of Compiègne was surrounded by Burgundian troops and when Joan arrived she joined up with soldiers from the French army who were there, trying to save it from being captured. (It was a bit like the situation at Orléans, but on a smaller scale.)

For several days there was sporadic fighting in the surrounding villages. Then one evening, as the church-bells were ringing, Joan rode out in front of her men on a dapple-grey horse – 'very beautiful and fiery', she later remembered.

They tried to sneak through a wood and surprise the Burgundians who were camped on the other side. Things didn't go according to plan, though, and the French were soon outnumbered.

They galloped at full speed back to Compiègne, but before they could all get across the drawbridge they were cut off. To protect the town, the drawbridge had to be raised, leaving Joan and a few others stranded in the soggy mud on the wrong side of the river.

Joan was soon surrounded by enemy soldiers, and she quickly realized there was no escape. A moment later a hulking great Burgundian soldier grabbed her by her cloak and yanked her off her horse. As Joan lay sprawling in the mud she no doubt gave her enemies a piece of her mind, but there was nothing she could do.

Back in the headlines

Word of Joan's capture spread fast. It was headline news, though the French and the English saw it slightly differently. . .

THE GALLIC GLOBE

24th May 1430

ZUT ALORS!

Magnificent Maid meets her match!

The Maid of Orléans has been taken from us! Joan, the People's Princess, is today languishing in a prison cell. She was captured by the enemy early last night after a magnificent display of heroism outside Compiègne.

The Angel of Light, 18, rose from an obscure background to rescue France in a time of dire need. She put our king where he is today.

This a black day for France. They've made off with our Maid! (How will we get her back?)

THE DAILY CHAIN MAIL

24th May 1430

GOTCHA!

FRENCH WITCH SEIZED IN TWILIGHT SWOOP

The monster who calls herself the 'Maid of Orléans' has been captured at last. In a daring and carefully planned manoeuvre, our Burgundian allies last night seized the French witch, otherwise known as the 'Limb of the Fiend', outside Compiègne.

The Handmaiden of Satan, 18, has for more than a year been terrorizing our brave lads in their noble efforts to civilize the French barbarians. But Englishmen everywhere can sleep easier in their beds tonight. The evil, wicked witch is behind bars at last. (And it won't be long before she fries!)

Although they hadn't heard much from Joan in the last few months, the English were still *desperate* to get their revenge on the Maid. They hadn't forgotten Orléans, or the battles that followed. Of course, they hadn't got their hands on her yet, and it would be a while before they prised her away from their slippery allies. . .

Who gets the girl?

The big Burgundian bloke who'd pulled Joan off her horse must have thought he'd won the lottery at first. As we know, prisoners could be traded in for cash, and the Maid was the Biggest Catch Of Them All. It must have been a terrible let-down when he remembered he had to surrender his priceless prisoner to his lord, the one-eyed John of Luxembourg.

John of Luxembourg's lord was Philip the Good himself, and he was the one who ultimately had to decide what to do with her. Of course, he wasn't as friendly with the English as he used to be. (He'd swapped sides a couple of times recently, when Charles had offered deals.) So he wasn't just going to hand her over to the English at the drop of a hat. He'd make them bargain for her.

For the time being, Philip decided to let John look after Joan. And when he knew she was safely under lock and key, he couldn't resist coming to have a look at the strange young girl who'd given him such grief and dared to write to him in that uppity way.

It wasn't long before Phil started getting letters about Joan, from various other people who wanted to get their hands on her:

PARIS
26 May 1430

Dear Mr 'The Good',

A little birdy has told us that you have captured that wretched girl— you know, the lippy one who's caused all the bother. Well, we all think you should send her to us so we can try her as a heretic and get rid of her once and for all. (It will of course be a <u>completely fair</u> trial.)

Yours sincerely,

Churchmen of Paris University

If they'd had University Challenge in those days this lot would probably have been world champions as long as all the questions were about theology (religious know-how).

The University of Paris was where some of the most important churchmen in the land hung out and stayed up late arguing over the right way to worship God.

At a time when people weren't sure which pope to believe in, the Paris theologians thought *they* were the only people who really knew what was what when it came to matters of the Church. They always kept their beady eyes out for people who didn't believe what the Church said they should believe. They called these people 'heretics' and tried to stamp them out.

The Paris churchmen were a bit like the churchmen Joan had once had to deal with at Poitiers, except *these* churchmen weren't supporters of the King of France like they were. These churchmen supported the English, instead. (The English had offered them loads of cushy jobs to keep them sweet. Those who opposed the English had been chucked out, though, and some of them had gone to Poitiers.) As a result, these churchmen weren't just a teeny bit suspicious of Joan, like the ones at Poitiers: this lot really hated her.

The churchmen were scared Philip might do something stupid like give Joan back to the French in return for a big fat ransom. So they piled on the pressure...

There was one man in particular – Pierre Cauchon, the Bishop of Beauvais – who made it his business to see that Joan got punished. In fact, Cauchon brought his own letters to Philip, asking for Joan to be given to him personally.

Cauchon was no longer a member of Paris University, but he still kept in touch with his old pals, and agreed with them completely about Joan. The Burgundians had originally made him bishop as a reward for being so loyal to them after the Treaty of Troyes, but now he was even more matey with the English, and especially with the regent, Bedford. So he was well in with Joan's enemies, and had his own reasons for hating her. . .

• His home city was Rheims, and he was gutted to see it back in the hands of the French. *He blamed Joan.*

- He was a top Church peer, and *hated* the idea that Charles had been crowned at Rheims with the help of a bunch of makeshift, phoney VIPs. *He blamed Joan.*
- He'd been kicked out of Beauvais when the town had surrendered to Charles's army a few months before. *He blamed Joan.*

Cauchon had fled to Paris and then sucked up to his English pals until they'd offered him another job as bishop near Rouen. From there, he'd plotted his revenge – if only he could get his hands on her. Luckily for him, Joan had been captured not far from his old stamping-ground at Beauvais and he thought that was reason enough to be put in charge of her trial.

Cauchon knew how much the English leaders wanted to see the Maid get her comeuppance, so it wasn't hard for him to persuade his mate Bedford to offer the Burgundians some cash.

John of Luxembourg and Philip the Good had a choice. Either they could keep Joan, and perhaps try to get a ransom for her from the French, or else sell her to the English if the price was right.

They thought about it for months, while Joan remained a prisoner.

JOAN ALONE

Soon after her capture Joan was moved to a castle not far away where she was locked up in a fifty-foot tower. Her servant John had been captured with her and at first they were imprisoned together. As they sat in their cell at the top of the tower, Joan must have told him how she'd feared the battle at Compiègne might be her last.

NICE VIEW THOUGH...

The great escape (nearly)

Being Joan, though, she didn't just sit around being depressed. She soon got busy with an escape-plan. She pulled up the planks on the floor of her cell, and, because she was fairly small, she was able to squeeze through the rafters into the room below. Luckily, it wasn't locked and she sneaked out into the corridor. She was just about to lock the guards in their own guard room, when she was spotted and banged up once again.

This time she was thrown in a dark cell, all alone. She'd never see her servant or any of her friends again.

Later she was asked about her escape attempt. Wasn't it wrong of her to try to escape if her voices had told her she was going to be captured? Wasn't she going against God's wishes? 'Poppycock!' said Joan. If she saw a chance to escape she would jolly well take it, because...

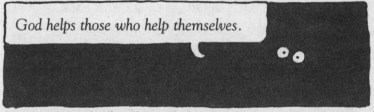

Joan's voices had only said she would be captured. They hadn't said what would happen after that, and Joan always hoped that God had plans for her to get away somehow.

Charles to the rescue?

Even if she couldn't escape by herself, Joan still hoped that someone might help her.

> JOAN'S SECRET DIARY
> June 1430
> I wonder what Charles is up to. Hmmm...
> I expect he's busy planning a rescue
> attempt, bless him. He'll be missing

It's sad to think of Joan dreaming like this, because in actual fact the chances of Charlie saving the day were absolutely zero. If Joan was now a damsel in distress, Charles was no knight-in-shining-armour, and he was much too cautious to try anything daring like a rescue. In fact, he was partly relieved to see the back of Joan, who'd always been a bit of a handful for him.

Ordinary people all over France were devastated at the news of Joan's capture – especially at Orléans, where special prayers were said for the Maid – but there wasn't much they could do without Charles's help. There was vague talk of a ransom but Charles was flat broke as usual, and couldn't be bothered to try and raise the necessary money.

He didn't absolutely rule it out, but rescuing Joan wasn't his highest priority.

Things to do

1. Have a lie in.
2. Run a nice hot bath.
3. Try on crown again and prance about in front of mirror.
4. Have a rest.
5. Settle down with plate of croissants while listening to nobles telling me what a wise and noble king I am.
6. Have another rest.
7. Have a little think about one day rescuing Joan. (Could leave this till tomorrow.)

Charles did get round to sending a messenger to Luxembourg, asking him not to give her to the English, but that was about it. He didn't actually do anything. Frankly, he couldn't really care less what happened to her.

Maximum security

Joan was a high-profile prisoner, and her enemies were terrified she might get away. So, before long, they moved her further north to a much stronger prison at a castle called Beaurevoir.

165

Beaurevoir was where Luxembourg lived and Joan soon met his family – his wife, his aunt, and his step-daughter – all of whom she quite liked. They felt sorry for Joan and tried to cheer her up by making her feel at home as much as possible.

They also tried to get Joan to chuck away her men's clothing and put on a dress. They pointed out that she wouldn't be riding any horses in prison, and there was no need for her to dress as a man – it just made everyone think she was weird.

But Joan said she wouldn't dump her boy's stuff till she had permission from her voices. She told them that if she *was* going to wear a dress (which she wasn't), she'd rather take one from them than from anyone else in France. She was trying to be polite, because she liked these women and thought they meant well, but she was absolutely determined to hang on to the trousers and shirt she'd got so used to wearing.

Despite her stubbornness the women still liked Joan. In fact they were so impressed with her that they begged Luxembourg not to hand her over to the English. They knew she'd get no mercy there, and didn't like to think about what might happen to her. But it was no use, because in the end Philip the Good told Luxembourg he must do a deal with Cauchon and the English.

167

Cauchon had persuaded his mate Bedford to offer the Burgundians a huge bag of money, and it was this that finally swung it.

Joan gets jumpy

When Joan learned about the deal, she was horrified...

<u>JOAN'S SECRET DIARY</u>

Beaurevoir, October 1430

DAY 63

My worst nightmare's about to come true. They're selling me to the English! It'll be much harder to rescue me when I'm in an English prison further north. And the English hate me even more than the Burgundians do. They want to kill me, I know it.

My voices said a very strange thing today. 'Joan, whatever you do, <u>don't</u> jump off the roof.' Of course I won't jump off the roof. It hadn't even occurred to me. What a stupid idea!

DAY 70

Why won't Charles help me? What's keeping him? He'd better get a move on or it'll

be too late.
 Voices came, but only told me not to jump off the roof, again!

DAY 74

 A guard has just told me that Compiègne is about to be overrun by Burgundians. He says they're going to massacre all the townspeople. I feel sick. Everything's going wrong. Where *is* Charles?
 All my voices ever say is the same thing — don't jump off the roof!

DAY 80

Charles isn't coming, is he? I realize that now. Oh well. I suppose he has his reasons.
 Was thinking of Mum today, and all my friends at home. It's so long since I've seen them. Domrémy seems like another world. How did I get from there to... this?
 The guards are coming. It must be time for my daily walk.

169

Every day Joan was taken for a breath of fresh air – on the roof of the castle tower where she was kept. On this particular day she suddenly decided to do exactly what her voices had told her *not* to do.

Somehow Joan survived her jump, despite falling more than 20 metres. She was fairly small and light, and perhaps there were bushes to break her fall. At any rate, when the guards retrieved her crumpled body she was cut and bruised, but hadn't broken any bones. She was badly concussed and when she realized where she was she went into a blinding rage before bursting into tears. Then she was carried back to her cell. For several days she ate nothing, and hardly spoke.

When Joan was asked about her jump later on she gave more than one explanation. First she said she'd jumped because she was afraid of being a prisoner of the English, and because she felt she'd rather die than hear about more Frenchmen killed at Compiègne. Joan had never actually disobeyed her voices before, and she must have struggled desperately with her urge to jump. (In a strange way, though, her voices seem to have put the idea in her head in the first place.)

MEDIEVAL MATTERS

Suicide

To try to kill yourself was considered a very serious sin in those days. If you succeeded you weren't allowed to be buried in holy ground. You were throwing away what only God could give – your life – and people thought that even He might not be able to forgive that.

Later, Joan seemed to change her mind about the reason for her jump. She now said that, in fact, she'd just been trying to escape:

I did not do it out of despair, but in the hope of saving my body and going to help some good people who were in need.

To be honest, this sounds unlikely. Joan must have known that the fall was potentially lethal and that she had little or no chance of getting through the heart of Burgundian territory without any help, not even a horse. It's hard to see the jump from the tower as anything other than the act of a desperate person.

If it was, imagine how guilty Joan must have felt when she realized what she'd done. Her voices, from that day forth, kept telling her she had to ask God to forgive her.

171

No wonder she later tried to pretend she'd just been trying to escape. She probably didn't even want to admit to herself what she'd done.

Au revoir to Beaurevoir

When John of Luxembourg heard what had happened he was really, really upset: if anything happened to Joan he'd lose his cash! So as soon as she'd recovered from her injuries he packed her off to Arras, where she'd be the responsibility of the Duke of Burgundy. Let *him* look after her until the English were ready to put her on trial.

At Arras the Duke of Burgundy sent men to Joan to persuade her to take off her men's clothes and wear a dress. Again Joan declined the offer. . .

Here, Joan was allowed occasional visits from well-wishers – including a Scotsman who brought a picture he'd made of Joan in armour, kneeling before King Charles. Other visitors must have tried to give Joan something more useful because one day she was caught hiding a stash of files – for filing away her prison bars. Unfortunately they were discovered before she had a chance to use them. And, at Arras, Joan was lucky enough to find another priest – a fellow-prisoner who'd been arrested for siding with King Charles – and she was allowed to confess to him and take communion.

Prison life was about to get a whole lot worse, though, because at Christmas Joan was on the way to the English headquarters at Rouen.

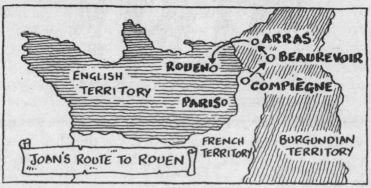

A BEAUTIFUL TRIAL

Once the English got their hands on Joan, there was no way they were going to let her live, but they had to set up a big trial to make everything look legal and above board.

She hadn't actually committed any obvious *crimes*, of course, except for beating them in battles. So the English planned to have her tried on *religious* grounds, which is where Cauchon came in. If she was found guilty of heresy, they could justify finishing her off. They also hoped to convince *themselves* that what they'd always said about Joan – that she was a witch – was actually true. Then they wouldn't feel so bad about killing her.

And if they could officially 'prove' to the world that Joan was a heretic or a witch then it gave them an extra weapon to use against King Charles of France. They could tell everyone he'd been helped to his crown by an evil creature of the Devil (or 'Limb of the Fiend') and therefore persuade people – even his own followers – that he wasn't a proper king, anointed by God.

THE ROUEN TIMES

1st January 1431

THE TRIAL OF THE CENTURY

Preparations are under way for what will surely be the trial of the century! Townspeople were eager to catch a glimpse of the celebrity prisoner when she arrived yesterday. It isn't every day you get to see a witch!

Pierre Cauchon, the Bishop of Beauvais, is in charge of the trial. With a doctorate in theology and a gigantic chip on his shoulder, he's a man well qualified for the job. Having finally got his hands on the teenage tearaway, Cauchon is said to be beside himself with excitement – after all, this trial is a bit special.

Cauchon has brought in a team of experts to help him: six bishops, 48 theologians and 110 other officials. He's certainly got a lot to do: prepare his evidence; find witnesses to speak against the accused; think of awkward questions; and select from his own team a panel of 'assessors' or judges whom he can rely on to give a guilty verdict. He was determined, he said yesterday, *'to make a beautiful trial of this'*.

For Cauchon, a beautiful trial was one where everything was done properly (i.e. his way). The English kept telling him to get a move on – they couldn't get rid of Joan soon enough. He was more methodical, though, and didn't care if his trial went on for ages so long as it was 'beautiful'.

Cauchon had asked someone called the Vice-Inquisitor to help him, because a trial like this was valid only if an important chap from the Inquisition was present. (The Inquisition was the part of the Church in charge of making sure people believed only what the Church said they should believe.) The Vice-Inquisitor wasn't much interested at first – he could see the trial was going to be a complete stitch-up and wanted no part of it. But he was told he had no choice, so he turned up in the end.

Cauchon's first step was to send a team of investigators off to Domrémy to nose around and try to dig up some dirt on Joan. Surely they could find some nasty gossip? Something to prove what an evil witch she'd always been. But his men came back empty-handed: no one in Domrémy had a bad word to say about Joan! One of the investigators said he'd found out nothing that he wouldn't wish to find out about his own sister.

Meanwhile. . .

Imprisoned at Rouen castle, Joan was badly treated. The only furniture in her cell was an iron bed, to which she was chained. Whenever she was allowed to leave her cell she was guarded closely and forced to wear leg-irons, which gave her terrible blisters. The English even made a hideous iron contraption – a sort of body-cage designed to keep Joan absolutely still. They were probably just trying to frighten her, though, because although they put it in her cell, they didn't actually use it.

JOAN'S SECRET DIARY

Rouen, February 1431

I've been here for nearly two months now and the trial hasn't even started yet.

It's awful here, and there isn't any privacy. Some of my guards are actually locked in the cell with me, and there are others outside. They all tease me horribly, and they're vicious and cruel. One minute they say I'm about to be freed and the next they tell me I'm about to be executed. I think they do it just to make me cry.

The strange thing is, I think they're actually a little afraid of me. They're simple men, who've heard all the stories about me being a witch – and here they are locked up with me!

Yesterday a tailor arrived with orders to measure me up for a dress. I didn't have much choice (though I'm determined not to wear it). But then he tried to touch me so I shouted and slapped him hard. That showed him.

ow!

The battle of wits begins

At the end of February 1431 Joan's trial really got going.

First, as at most trials, she was asked to swear that she'd tell the whole truth. This was usually just a routine matter, but Joan replied:

> *But I do not know what you will ask me about. Perhaps you will ask me things which I shall not tell you.*

Joan made it very clear there were some things she wasn't prepared to discuss, even in court. (She meant her voices.) Her accusers quickly realized they had a tough customer on their hands.

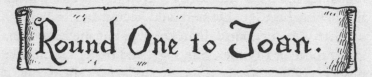

Round One to Joan.

Next Joan was taken to a large room packed with 44 unfriendly 'assessors' ready to put their questions to her. She sat at a table facing them, all alone at one end of the room. Two notaries – or clerks – made official notes. (These brief notes made during the trial were written up properly each evening.)

179

Joan was asked all about her family background and her upbringing. Cauchon, who led the questioning, asked her to repeat the Lord's Prayer, to check she knew it. (If not, he thought, he could accuse her of being a witch!) Well, of course, Joan knew it, but she wasn't just going to say it to order. She suggested he let her make a proper confession to a priest and *then* she'd say it properly!

Round Two to Joan.

Next Cauchon warned her that if she tried to escape, that would only prove she was a heretic since God had obviously willed that she be put on trial. But Joan didn't believe a word of it. If she saw a chance to escape, she told him, she'd be out of there and no mistake. She even dared to complain in public about her prison conditions and about being 'chained in these iron hobbles'.

Round Three to Joan.

If at first you don't succeed . . . cheat!

So far Cauchon wasn't doing very well, but he had one or two cards up his sleeve.

Sneaky plan A

1. Send priest to Joan's cell, pretending to be on her side.

> 2. Leave men outside cell to write down anything incriminating she might say.

At first Joan liked the priest, and soon got him to hear her in confession. He pretended to be a fellow prisoner and she thought he was a friend . . . until one day she actually saw him in court, joining in with the questioning!

Sneaky plan B

Hide two of my men behind curtain in court. Get them to write their own set of notes. (Tell them only to write down things that will help our case and ignore anything else Joan says.)

SCRIBBLE

Later, accuse the official notaries of being biased in favour of Joan and <u>adding</u> things to their notes.

Fortunately, the official notaries weren't frightened of Cauchon and told him to get stuffed. They said Cauchon had better let them do their job properly or they'd tell everyone what a dirty cheat he was.

Ask a silly question

In the sessions that followed, Cauchon and his men fired question after question at Joan, for hours and hours on end. They planned to wear her down until she said something suspicious – it didn't much matter what – and then they'd use it to cook up some charges against her.

So Joan was asked again and again about every part of her life: her childhood in Domrémy; her journeys to Vaucouleurs and then to Chinon; her adventures at Orléans; the coronation at Rheims; the disaster at Paris; right up to her capture at Compiègne and her attempts to escape from prison.

The questions came thick and fast, and sometimes several of Cauchon's men spoke at once so that Joan had to tell them:

Please, good sirs, one at a time!

They kept interrupting Joan too, not letting her finish one answer before asking her something else.

On the whole, Joan gave her accusers straight answers, but when they asked about her voices, she often said. . .

PASS!

There were some things Joan felt were none of their business, and she told them she'd never speak about her voices even if they cut off her head. (It didn't make sense, but everyone knew what she meant!) And once, when Cauchon asked what her voices had been saying to her in prison, Joan said they'd told her some gossip about him but she wasn't going to tell him what it was!

But as the trial went on she did begin to say more and more about her voices, explaining for example that they were St Michael, St Catherine and St Margaret. But the assessors were never satisfied, and the questions about her voices just got sillier and sillier. . .

The more physical Joan made her voices sound, the less her judges liked them, even though it was their stupid questions that forced her to describe them like that in the first place.

You're *sure* you're not a witch?

Sometimes Joan's interrogators would pursue one line of questioning for ages and then suddenly change the subject to try and trick Joan into saying something that would get her into trouble.

Cauchon and his men were absolutely desperate to get Joan to admit she was a witch. So they kept asking her about the Fairies' Tree at Domrémy. Wasn't all this stuff about fairies extremely suspicious? Hadn't Joan and her

1. A mandrake is a plant that witches were supposed to carry with them.

friends actually 'consorted with fairies', they asked her and didn't that show that she was in touch with evil spirits even when she was little?

But they were out of luck. Joan just wasn't buying it.

> WE WERE JUST PLAYING. THE FACT IS, I'M NOT A WITCH. AND THAT'S ALL THERE IS TO IT!

Joan gets the upper hand

Again and again, Cauchon's men tried to trick Joan with cunning questions designed to trap her. . .

> ARE YOU IN A STATE OF GRACE?

> AN EXCELLENT QUESTION. HE MEANS IS SHE SURE SHE'S BEEN SAVED BY GOD. SHE'LL EITHER HAVE TO ADMIT SHE'S DAMNED OR SAY 'YES' AND THEN WE CAN ACCUSE HER OF PRESUMING TO KNOW WHAT'S IN GOD'S MIND. SHE CAN'T WIN. TEE HEE!

But Joan was on her toes, and wasn't going to be caught out so easily. . .

If I am not, may God put me in it; and if I am, may God keep me in it.

Joan must have been exhausted by all this, but for the most part she kept her cool and gave as good as she got. Sometimes, when she heard a question for the third or fourth time, she'd tell her judges to look back at her previous answers. She wasn't going to go through it all again. She even told them that she'd already answered some questions about her voices when Charles had sent her to the bishops at Poitiers, and that they should look up the answers she gave then.

At one point, though, Joan did lose her temper and told Cauchon outright that he had no right to set himself up as her judge.

THE ROUEN TIMES

7th March 1431

'WITCH' WINS FRIENDS AS TRIAL HITS TROUBLE

The trial of the century is not going according to plan. 'The accused' may even get off scot-free unless someone can actually think of something to accuse her of!

And the accused's replies grow more cheeky by the hour. Asked whether God had told her to wear men's clothes, she said the question of her clothes wasn't important and her judges shouldn't concern themselves with it.

Asked once again what her voices had said to her recently, she merely replied: 'That I should answer you boldly.' And when one of her previous answers was read back to her by one of the notaries she told him he'd made a mistake and threatened to 'pull his ears' if he didn't pay more attention.

Notary: must try harder

Replies like these are provoking laughter in the courtroom, and one or two of her judges are even beginning to grow fond of the accused.

Bishop Cauchon was yesterday reported to be furious with one of his own men because he admitted he could not blame Joan anything she said.

The case continues.

Joan had once admitted that she didn't 'know A from B' (i.e. she couldn't read or write), but she was clearly no fool. Without a lawyer to help her, or even a friend to advise and support her, an illiterate girl was getting the better of the learned doctors who were so determined to see her destroyed.

At one point, a famous legal expert was passing through town. Cauchon showed him the trial record to see what he thought. The expert said the trial wasn't fair because Joan had been given no list of the accusations against her and because it was obvious that most of her judges hated her and *intended* to convict her. He thought the whole thing was a scandal and said he couldn't bear to watch it. He left soon after.

Cauchon changes tactics

After about a week of questioning, Cauchon decided Joan was taking advantage of all the attention she was getting in the courtroom and she was winning far too much sympathy. Cauchon thought he might have more luck if he conducted the trial in private. So, for the next two weeks, he and just a handful of his most trusted men interrogated Joan in her tiny cell where she couldn't get the better of them so easily.

Cauchon also changed his line of attack, now concentrating on asking awkward questions about episodes she'd sooner forget. He hoped to make her feel as guilty as possible about some of the things she'd done. Why *had* she attacked Paris on a holy day? Why *had* she broken her promise and let that Burgundian prisoner be killed? Why *had* she jumped from the tower at Beaurevoir, even though her voices had told her not to? He even tried to make her squirm by reminding her she'd stolen the bishop of Senlis's horse!

JOAN'S SECRET DIARY
Rouen, March 1431

It's awful. Now I'm actually locked in with those horrible old men and their horrid, horrid questions. The same ones over and over again. 'Why did you do this? Why did you do that. Why? Why? Why?' Are they trying to drive me mad?

Today they asked me why I'd encouraged my army to kill so many men. I told them I preferred my standard 40 times more than my sword and that I never killed any man on purpose, even in battle. But I'm not sure they believed it. (I'm not sure I believe it myself.)

Joan was getting worn out and depressed, and she soon started to get more careless. Her judges asked her again about her first meeting with Charles: had there been a golden angel above his head? When they'd asked this before, she'd dismissed the idea: 'By Mary,' she'd said, 'if there was one I never saw it!' But now she was tired, and ended up saying that yes there *had* been a golden angel. She described in great detail how it had appeared to her at Chinon and placed a golden crown on Charles's head so that she was able to recognize him. It was just a way of speaking, really, and a way of describing her own certainty about Charles. But her judges thought someone who claimed to see golden angels was *highly* suspicious (even though it was they who had first mentioned it!).

Playing with words
Joan was soon to find herself in more difficulties. . .

<u>JOAN'S SECRET DIARY</u>

Cauchon's up to his old tricks again. Now he keeps asking me if I'll 'submit to the Church'. He must have asked me 20 times or more. I kept saying, 'No, I will submit only to God.' I thought Cauchon and his bishops thought they <u>were</u> the Church. I thought he was asking if I agreed with them that I'm a heretic.

But then I realized I'd been falling right into his trap. The Church is much bigger than that. Cauchon and his henchmen are only one little part of it. My voices have never said anything against the Church as a whole and personally I <u>love</u> going to church. So I should have been saying 'Yes'. By saying 'No' it looked like I was saying I didn't agree with the Church at all and was admitting to being a heretic!

Eventually a friendly assessor advised Joan to say that she did submit to the Church, but not to the bit of it represented by the churchmen from Paris University. Joan told Cauchon she submitted to God and the Pope in Rome, and it was hard for Cauchon to argue with that. He got really angry, though, and told the notaries not to record Joan's reply! For that, he got a ticking off from Joan:

Ha! You write well enough what goes against me, and yet you do not write what is for me.

The accused accused at last

Joan was now taken back to court where a list of 70 accusations was finally read to her.

IS THAT ALL YOU COULD COME UP WITH?

RIFFLE

(You might expect a trial to begin with accusations, with the accused then being questioned about them. This one began with loads of questions and then the accusations were cobbled together at the end!)

191

Many of the charges were obviously complete nonsense, and referred to things which Joan had already explicitly denied. (That she carried a mandrake, for example, and had uttered magic spells while melting candle wax on to the heads of children!) Joan pointed out how unfair many of the charges were and Cauchon eventually whittled them down to 12 main ones. These weren't very fair either, though. (For example, Joan was *still* accused of not properly submitting to the Church.)

Mainly, the charges focused on her voices and the way she listened to them more than to the Church. But they also brought up the Golden Angel she'd said she'd seen at Chinon, her habit of making prophecies, her men's clothes, her suicide attempt, and the fact she'd disobeyed her parents when she ran away from home in the first place.

Cauchon passed round the 12 charges and sent them to his pals at the University of Paris for their learned opinion.

More dirty tricks

Even on Easter day, the holiest day of the year, Joan still wasn't allowed to go to mass or take communion. Cauchon said he'd only let her if she agreed to wear women's clothes from now on. (He was becoming more and more obsessed with her men's clothes, and hoped to convict her for wearing them.) Joan wouldn't accept this. She said she'd put on a dress just for mass, but would then return to her men's clothes. Cauchon said no, that wasn't good enough.

Then Joan became ill, and accused Cauchon of deliberately poisoning her. In fact, though, she'd probably just eaten some prison food that was past its sell-by date. Cauchon wanted her dead, but only as a result of his beautiful trial. Bumping her off on the quiet just wasn't his style.

When she was better, Cauchon continued the questioning, hoping Joan might still say something to convict herself more clearly. But in April Joan told him it was no use asking her any more stupid questions:

I will not do or say anything other than what I have said before.

So Cauchon decided it was time to show her something he thought might change her mind ... the torture chamber.

In fact, Cauchon's top men had voted by 11 votes to 2 *not* to torture Joan. But Cauchon was probably hoping he might scare Joan enough just by showing her his

193

fancy torture kit. As usual, though, he underestimated his prisoner and Joan's response was typical:

> *Truly, if you tear my limbs away and separate my soul from my body, I shall not say anything different to you; and if I do say something, then afterwards I will always tell people that you forced me to say it.*

The verdict from Paris

In May, the University of Paris sent back its conclusions. They said Joan was obviously 'blasphemous towards God' and seriously 'in error as to the faith'. And they decided her voices must be either 'fictions of human invention' or things that 'proceeded from an evil spirit'.

Cauchon's men then explained why it was impossible to believe her voices were from God. . .

IF A KING PUT SOMEONE IN CHARGE OF A FORTRESS AND TOLD HIM NOT TO LET ANYONE IN...

...AND THEN SOMEONE CAME AND SAID HE WAS FROM THE KING AND WANTED TO BE LET IN...

...THEN THAT PERSON, BEFORE BEING LET IN, WOULD HAVE TO PROVE HE REALLY WAS FROM THE KING.

What they meant was: God has put the Church in charge of religion on earth and if someone like Joan comes along and says she has direct word from God, then it's up to her to *prove* it.

But Joan wasn't going to be forced into 'proving' her voices existed – she had always made it clear that she didn't do miracles. Equally, she wasn't going to change her mind and say they didn't exist. She just stuck to her guns:

> *If I were to be condemned, and saw the fire lit, I would say nothing different.*

Unfortunately, Joan's courage and determination couldn't last much longer.

Joan gives in

With the verdict from Paris, Cauchon now thought he probably had all he needed to convict Joan, but first he wanted to humiliate her in public. So, at the end of May, her head was shaved and she was forced to wear a dress. Then she was taken to a cemetery outside the castle walls and everyone was invited to come and jeer at her. . .

To the terrified, exhausted Joan, the cheering crowds of Orléans and Rheims must have seemed a very long way away now. While the Rouen crowd hurled abuse at her the priest repeated that if she signed she would be saved, and if she didn't she'd be burned straight away.

Exhausted from months of terrifying imprisonment, and weeks of gruelling questioning, Joan was now at her wits' end. She was only human, after all, and finally she gave in and with the help of the priest she signed the paper.

We don't know exactly what the paper said (and neither did Joan). It probably said that she admitted she'd been wrong about her voices being from God, that she would chuck away her men's clothing, and submit to the Church. Joan was in such a state by now she probably didn't *care* what it said.

Armed with the Facts

Joan's signature

Witnesses say Joan signed with a cross, something that people who couldn't write often did in those days. But we know that Joan *could* write her own name (though nothing else) because she signed many of the letters she dictated. Sometimes, though, she'd signed a letter with a cross as a sort of codeword to let the person know that she didn't mean what she said in the letter. (She would do this if she thought the enemy were going to get their hands on it, to trick them.) When Joan signed the priest's bit of paper with a cross it might have been like making a promise with crossed fingers.

For the English, all this was a terrible let-down. The whole point of the trial had been to show what a shocking heretic Joan was and how she fully deserved to go up in smoke a.s.a.p. But now she'd been given a way out. She'd agreed that she'd been wrong and had asked to be guided by the Church. That was bad news because, according to the rules of the Inquisition, you couldn't burn a heretic if they admitted they were wrong. You could only punish them with boring old life imprisonment!

Thinking they were going to miss out on a sing-song round the fire, the English were *furious* with Cauchon for letting Public Enemy Number One off the hook. After all this time, it looked like the bungling old bishop had botched his 'beautiful trial'.

Joan changes her mind

Heretics who admitted they were wrong were supposed to be kept in church prisons, where conditions were less harsh. Joan demanded to be moved, but Cauchon refused and sent her straight back to the English prison she loathed so much.

JOAN'S SECRET DIARY
Thursday, 24th May 1431

What have I done? What have I done? It's only just sinking in. Can God ever forgive me?

The guards taunt me for giving in and wearing a dress, but that's nothing compared with my voices, who keep reminding me how I've betrayed them, and betrayed God.

So what have I got to look forward to now? A lifetime chained up in this horrid prison, abandoned even by God. I can't live with that, I'd rather die.

After a few days, though, Joan was wearing men's clothes once again. According to one story, she didn't have much choice, because while she was sleeping her guards took away her dress and left a pile of men's stuff instead. Well, Joan had to wear *something* when she got up...

Anyway, as soon as Cauchon heard that she'd gone back on her promise he went straight to her cell. Joan told him that to be honest she felt safer in men's clothes when she was among her English prison guards. Then she told him she preferred to wear men's clothes *anyway* and had actually *decided* to put them on again because her voices were so disappointed with her. Finally, she told him that her voices were real and that if she'd ever said otherwise she now regretted it.

Though he pretended to be sorry, Cauchon was delighted. This was exactly what he'd hoped for. (He may have actually *wanted* her to sign the paper in the cemetery, knowing that she'd soon change her mind, which would make it easier to have her burned.) In going back to her old ways, Joan had proved once and for all that she was a *completely* hopeless heretic who was hell-bent on disobeying the Church and deserved to die. Cauchon could hand her over to the English executioner with a clear conscience.

When he left Joan's cell, after she'd told him her decision, Cauchon bumped into an important English earl in the corridor. He slapped the earl on the shoulder and said:

Be of good heart. It is done.

A HORRIBLE END

Three days later, in her cell, Joan admitted to her judges that she had made up the story about the golden angel at Chinon who had pointed to King Charles. 'I was the angel and there was no other,' she said. The angel had just been a way of describing her own sense of certainty about which person the king was, which she felt must have been inspired by God.

About her voices, though, Joan said, 'Whether they were good or evil spirits, they appeared to me.'

Joan didn't know exactly what awaited her that day but she must have had an idea. She said she believed that by evening she would be in Paradise.

When Joan was told that she was about to be burned at the stake she burst into tears. Seized with terror, she said:

Alas. Am I to be treated so horribly?

When Cauchon visited her cell Joan screamed at him: 'I die because of you!'

He replied that it was her own fault for returning to her witchcraft and her old ways. (She had 'relapsed' into heresy – just as he'd hoped.) Then he let Joan make her confession and take communion.

Joan was put on a cart and taken to the old market-place in Rouen. There was another hostile reception from the hundreds of Rouen citizens who'd turned up to gawp at the execution.

Joan, who had herself called the Maid, a liar, pernicious deceiver of the people, sorceress, superstitious, blasphemer of God, defamer of the faith of Jesus Christ. boastful, idolatrous, cruel, dissolute, invoker of demons, apostate, schismatic and heretic.

THEY FORGOT 'WITCH'!

A preacher came on to the platform and preached another long sermon at Joan. She just listened, in a state of confusion and shock: did people really believe all those things about her? Cauchon told her she must think of her soul and hope that God would forgive her.

A paper hat was put on Joan's head with a label that said: 'Heretic, relapsed, apostate, idolater.'

Then Joan knelt down and prayed for half an hour, asking God to forgive her enemies. Many people in the crowd now wept tears of pity for Joan, who was, after all, just a 19-year-old girl facing an awful fate. But a circle of 200 English soldiers kept them away from the platforms, and jeered at her, as they'd done so many times before.

Joan was dragged to the stake and chained to it, while she cried in horror.

It was as though she still couldn't quite believe what was happening to her.

Joan asked if she might have a cross to hold, and an English soldier near by took pity on her and made one from a stick lying on the ground. He reached up and gave it to her and she held it tight.

A priest walked on to the scaffold where the stake was and tried to comfort Joan, but another English soldier stopped him, complaining that they'd all been waiting long enough for the execution to begin.

Eventually Joan's hands were tied, and the fire was lit. In a few minutes it was all over at last.

AFTER JOAN

In the years after Joan's death, King Charles didn't seem to miss her much, though some of his army captains certainly did. La Hire, Dunois and d'Alençon continued to fight for Charles but they never again experienced anything like those heady days with the Maid of Orléans. (In the end, d'Alençon fell out with Charles and actually ended up in prison after plotting against him.)

Charles's policy of making deals paid off in the end. He made a lasting peace with the Burgundians in 1435, and soon regained control of Paris. (He rode into the capital with Joan's faithful servant John, now free from captivity, walking by his side.)

Eventually, after a lot of wheeling and dealing, and quite a bit more fighting, the English finally left France for good in 1453. (Actually, they kept a couple of tiny bits of France even after this, but nothing very much.) Charles, who was still king, took most of the credit and had a special medal struck celebrating his great victory.

He might have been a bit hopeless when he started out, but the truth was that Charles had become a crafty and highly successful king, and he ruled France for 30 years after Joan died.

In 1450 Joan's mum, now living in Orléans, asked the Pope to order another trial to clear her daughter's name. King Charles was all in favour since he didn't like people going around with the idea that he'd got where he was today with the help of a witch. So in 1455 another batch of learned churchmen – ones who weren't in favour of the English, this time – went through the whole thing again. They soon saw that the original trial had been a fix and that Joan was, after all, innocent. In 1456 the original verdict against her was officially overturned, but it was a bit late for Joan, whose ashes had been dumped in the River Seine 25 years earlier.

WELL, YOU CAN'T HAVE EVERYTHING.

In 1903 the Church declared that Joan was now officially 'Venerable', and in 1920 it made her a saint.